MW01593715

Thanks so much for your
interest in Coaches Outreach.

God bless,
Tommy Maxwell

Eph. 3:14-21

Praise for

NOT SO FAST

"No one has more stories or tells better stories than Tommy Maxwell. And this book is full of them. But as you'll discover, the stories are part of a much larger story of how God leads a gifted and successful athlete to launch a national ministry called Coaches Outreach. This ministry understands that coaches have a unique platform to influence the next generation and for over three decades has provided spiritual support for them and their marriages. It's making a difference! Tommy introduced me to Coaches Outreach a little over twenty years ago and I consider it an honor and a privilege to play a role in this powerful ministry today."

PETE CHIOFALO
PRESIDENT, COACHES OUTREACH

"Tommy has had an outstanding career on the field as well as off the field. He was always an encourager to the players, be it an average player, good player, or even the underdog. He knows how to encourage an athlete. Coaches have their own hill to climb and Tommy encourages them to reach their dream."

GENE STALLINGS
HEAD COACH,
TEXAS A&M UNIVERSITY, RETIRED
COLLEGE FOOTBALL HALL OF FAME

"Tommy had a vision to equip coaches to lead kids. It started with a Bible study aimed at coaches, and it's incredible now to see the growth of Coaches Outreach. I'm so excited for this book that tells the story."

TOMMY COX
HIGH SCHOOL COACH
& MEMBER, HALL OF HONOR
TEXAS HIGH SCHOOL COACHES ASSOCIATION

i

"I'd take a bullet for Tommy. But I'd have to get in line. Coaches love Tommy Maxwell—and Janice. He's a people-magnet, with a deep Christian walk and a seasoned knowledge of Scripture. When Tommy puts his arm around you, you know he cares. And when he passes around the Super Bowl ring, it doesn't get past the second guy. He's got street cred and uses humor with his lessons, as simple as 'Don't be a knothead.' He's perfect to reach coaches for Christ."

TIM KILGORE
35 YEARS COACHING
23 YEARS WITH COACHES OUTREACH

"Tommy's love for Jesus and passion for football is something you will see and feel as you read his story. That combination made him a great teammate—and friend. His stories on and off the field will make you laugh and cry, and you'll understand why people enjoy being around him and hearing him speak. Enjoy my brother in Christ, Tommy Maxwell."

BRAD MILLS
MAJOR LEAGUE BASEBALL
COACH & MANAGER, RETIRED

"Tommy caught the vision of how coaches can impact the lives of their players and use the Bible to train them to be positive leaders. Coaches Outreach helps coaches grasp a much more important role than merely wins and losses. God has used all of Tommy's experiences to uniquely prepare him to start this powerful ministry. I highly recommend *NOT SO FAST* as an insight into the life of a humble servant of the Lord."

RAY HUFFINES
BUSINESS OWNER, SUPPORTER,
& FORMER CHAIRMAN OF THE
COACHES OUTREACH BOARD

"Tommy Maxwell has painted a very entertaining and down-to-earth picture of God's grace and faithfulness. In *NOT SO FAST*, Tommy's personal story from childhood to present day comes alive through humor, his athletic experience, his personal journey to finding the Savior, and a God-sent angel named Janice who came to be a vital piece of the puzzle. You'll watch a professional football player becomes a minister of the Gospel, then establishes and develops Coaches Outreach, which weathers the storms to grow from a handful of coach's Bible studies to a national ministry reaching many thousands of coaches and their wives, student athletes, and others on a daily basis. Reading this story of God's grace and one man's faithfulness to his Savior is truly inspiring and uplifting."

JAN HETHCOCK
FOUNDING HEAD OF ATHLETICS,
OAKS CHRISTIAN SCHOOL, RETIRED

"Tommy Maxwell's football career has crossed paths with many of my childhood heroes, men with names like Stallings, Unitas, Shula, Blanda, and Madden. He even has a Super Bowl ring and yet, I find the most intriguing and inspirational moments of Tommy's life have occurred since his time in the NFL. Do yourself a favor. Read his book. As your life crosses paths with Tommy's, I believe you'll find him to be a humble and authentic man of faith."

BILL BLANKENSHIP
HIGH SCHOOL & COLLEGE COACH,
39 YEARS

"*NOT SO FAST: The Story of Tommy Maxwell and Coaches Outreach* reveals Tommy as a unique individual who is compassionate, loving, humorous, energetic, intelligent, articulate, but above all, passionate. Initially his passion involved sports, most especially, football. Later it would expand to incorporate his wife 'Twirly Bird' and their two daughters in addition to an all-abiding faith in a Sovereign Lord. Twenty-five years ago, out of this mix and after several Not So Fast experiences, the Lord moved Tommy to establish his ministry, Coaches Outreach. Over the years it has grown from a single group of high school coaches in Austin to multiplied thousands across the United States. 'Great is thy faithfulness, Lord unto me.'"

BURK MURCHISON
AUTHOR, *HOLE IN THE ROOF*
TOMMY'S FRIEND AND ADVOCATE

"Tommy Maxwell is a leader of men both on and off the football field. Kristi and I attended a Coaches Outreach retreat in the mid 90's. We gained understanding of our coaching profession as a ministry during this retreat. In today's culture and atmosphere, coaches need encouragement as never before. Tommy has consistently made an impact on people's lives through Coaches Outreach. We are very thankful for his passion and dedication to this ministry."

GUS MALZAHN
HEAD COACH,
UNIVERSITY OF CENTRAL FLORIDA

NOT SO FAST

The Story of Tommy Maxwell
& Coaches Outreach

Tommy Maxwell
with Rod Butler

© 2023 Coaches Outreach, Inc. All rights reserved.

NOT SO FAST: The Story of Tommy Maxwell and Coaches Outreach

Edited by Howard Hicks

All Scripture is from the English Standard Version (ESV Bible) unless otherwise noted. The ESV does not use uppercase letters in its pronouns when referring to God. This book will reflect that formatting as well.

Quote from *Bebes and the Bear*, by Ron J. Jackson, Jr. published 2019 by Texas A&M University Press.

Quotes and references from "AGGIE ACHIEVER: Double duty earns Tommy Maxwell Texas A&M Hall of Fame Honors" by Clay Coppedge, Sun Sports Editor, Sunday Sun, The Williamson County Sun, published October 13, 1991.

Photograph of the Maxwell family by kristinjphotography.com

No part of this book may be reproduced or transmitted in any form or by any means, electronic or mechanical, including photocopying, recording, or by any information storage and retrieval system, without written permission from the author.

Jones High School photo used by permission of the district press office, Houston ISD.

Photos related to the Jones High School, Oilers/Titans, Colts, Raiders and the Cotton Bowl used by permission.

Every attempt was made to contact Texas A&M University for permission to use photos related to A&M.

ISBN: 979-8-9884210-0-9

TABLE OF CONTENTS

To Janice, my love.

Thank you, country girl, for your gentle encouragement and setting me straight when I get off the tracks. When God brought you to me, he brought my other half. I am complete with you and always will be, till death do us part.

FOREWORD

I first met Tommy Maxwell at a summer cookout hosted by the men of my hometown church. Here was a former professional football player everyone was in awe of and everyone wanted to meet. A big city sports hero had come to visit the small town of his wife. This event would prove to be God's providence to me.

On that warm summer evening I heard Tommy share not only his pastor's heart, but talk about hosting a Bible study for high school coaches in and around Austin, Texas.

Being a young coach myself, this piqued my interest. Tommy shared stories of coaches engaging in Bible studies with gospel-driven conversations at early Friday morning meetings. This eventually birthed the idea of summer marriage retreats, where coaching couples could relax, relate, and decompress, all while finding community and common ground in Christ. I fully understood the rigor of coaching and the toll it could take on families immersed in this high-pressure, highly visible career where coaches were readily critiqued and criticized.

Needless to say, I was hooked. I felt like a lifeline had been cast my way. For the very first time, I began to view my life's work as a true ministry.

Fast forward another year. My wife, Ella, and I were privileged to attend one of the coaches' marriage retreats. More than just teaching, a vision was cast, empowering coaching couples to not just survive, but thrive. We left with a new excitement, realizing the impact this ministry could have.

These were the humble beginnings of what would become a profound ministry to coaches across the nation. We would have the privilege of prayerfully walking alongside Tommy and his lovely wife, Janice, encouraging them to build this much needed outreach.

What began as a small Bible study with coaches, blossomed into a multi-state organization that equips coaches, their spouses, and their families. These are the stories of a life-changing ministry and the people who enabled it to flourish.

Donnie Snodgrass
Football/Track Coach
Lorena High School
Lorena, Texas 2022

PROLOGUE
TIME WELL SPENT

One day on the practice field at Texas A&M, I missed catching a pass.

Coach Stallings saw it. He sat high up in his tower watching two different fields at the same time. He clicked on his megaphone, pointed it in my direction and called out, in his booming voice, "Anyone can catch the easy ones!"

After practice he asked me again why I missed that pass. I had all kinds of excuses for him. Finally, he answered, "Sounds like a lot of excuses, Tommy. Why don't you just perform better?"

That stirred me up—made me mad, really mad. But I've never forgotten coach Stallings' question. I can still hear it.

"Why don't you just perform better?"

It changed my view on "performance" forever. We never become better with excuses. God has used great coaches and mentors to show me that—over and over. Truth be told, I actually love Coach Stallings for his tough questions. He made me a better person.

And, whether it's athletics, or work, or marriage, or whatever, our Creator gifts all of his children with abilities and with purpose.

Seeing and understanding his purpose should keep us from making excuses. It should help us "perform" life better, because we see God's purpose, unfolding with more and more of God's wisdom.

These last couple of years have been a long, tough season for me. I've had to learn to look up to our Creator, having spent a lot of time on my back with five separate operations. I've had to try to stay focused and remember that God had a plan for me. Thankfully, I wasn't alone in the fight.

Coach Gene Stallings would check up on me. Other coaches, and friends from Coaches Outreach (CO) would drop by or call. And many of them, especially the God-ordained mentors in my life, would say things like:

"Tommy, how's your book coming?"

"You are going to finish your book, aren't you, Tommy?"

Of course, the book I'm talking about is the one you hold in your hands. It's proof that I didn't give up, and I did push through with it. Whew, it feels good to say that! And I hope that you—and every reader—will enjoy the stories and insights I've put together here. It's a lot of work, making a book, but, as I said, I knew God had a purpose, and this time, I didn't want to miss the catch!

I guess the Lord gave me several reasons to tell my story.

My first was to tell my life story (and God's story through me) for my two daughters and six grandkids, Lezley Nugent (Kate, Marshall, Lilly) and Lauren Scott (Maxwell, Nolan, Ford). Each firstborn grandson has part of my name, by the way. Sweet daughters did that for good ol' Dad. I always wished my dad, or my mom, had written something down about their lives. That was the first pass I was hoping to complete: throwing this "ball" to my kids and grandkids.

And my second purpose, the second pass, was to point folks biblically to God's sovereign control and purpose in our lives. The more we understand God's sovereignty, or total control, the bigger and more gracious he becomes. That makes life so much more exciting and purposeful.

That means there are no coincidences with our Creator. None. That's what my good friend, Scott Henderson, reminded me constantly. If God gives us years to live, he prepares our "performances" so that we become better and more effective. No excuses. Right, Coach? Right, God?

"For we are his workmanship, created in Christ Jesus for good works, which God prepared beforehand, that we should walk in them" (Ephesians 2:10). That leaves no room for pride in our performance. God receives all the credit—all the glory—for anything we do that he prepares for us and he considers worthy.

Before you jump into *NOT SO FAST*, I need to thank some God-ordained, in-Christ brothers who have kept after me to "Finish that book, Tommy!": Burk Murchison (who gave me a handheld voice recorder to remember my thoughts), Wendell Housley and Gaddy Wells (A&M football buddies), Tommy Teague (CO Board friend), Ed Ruby (friend from former church), Bill Beard (Aggie friend) and Dan Mitchell (his counseling and practical advice). They were my "encouragement team." I'm also grateful to the late Gary Kitchens, a fellow teammate at A&M, a hilarious comedian, but also a no-nonsense, very sharp businessman. He helped me organize Coaches Outreach as an original board member. I can't wait to see him in heaven. And special thanks to a new great friend, Rod Butler, who stepped in to help me when I was very low. He's an author himself and a huge inspiration. But he's not just an author, he's a teacher (another great coach), who took my writing and showed me how to make it better. He kept saying that I was a naturally good writer. That inspiration grew as I wrote. He said that my writing sounded like me when I spoke. That's good, isn't it? It will be kinda like me and you, going through this story together. I like that.

So, welcome to my back porch. Come on in, sit down, and get comfortable, as the game—I mean the story—begins. And be sure you notice the sign that says:

WASTING TIME ON OUR BACK PORCH IS
CONSIDERED TIME WELL WASTED!

However, this is a book dedicated to God and his purposes in our lives, so your time reading will be, I pray, time well spent.

Tommy

Scan this QR Code for Tommy's sports videos and interviews.

CHAPTER 1
GREAT COACHING

COACHING CRISIS

There's a crisis in sports today. And it's not just challenging the sports world—it's threatening to tear it apart. I'm not just talking pro sports here. There's a crisis in college sports, high school sports, and even younger. It strikes at the heart of sports and the nature of competition itself. This earthquake is shaking up a group of men and women who are essential to sports. You could say they're the very heartbeat of the sports world. Who would that be? I'll tell you in case you're stumped. Coaches! Coaches have been and will always be critical in good, healthy competition.

But now, good men, good women, called to teach, challenge, and encourage athletes, are leaving their profession in growing numbers. This stretches and wears out the coaches left in the lurch. And the new coaches who step in often come from a different mindset, more concerned with end results than nurturing and encouragement.

I recently heard a Major League manager comment on where professional baseball is going. Speaking from a hurting heart, he said the manager (coach) used to run the team. The manager was in control. The manager focused on building a relationship with each player. As the coach, he knew each player's needs, talents, and potential. However, today, it's about what the management wants to happen, instead of inspiring each player to be the best he can be. And a critical element in being the best you can be as an athlete requires being the best team player you can be, not just producing statistics so you can stand out as an individual. So the crisis hits hard. That's why my focus, my life in professional sports and in ministry, has always seemed to narrow down to one group of very important people: coaches.

A GREAT COACH

I've always appreciated and admired great coaching. I've always seen coaching as more than just wins and losses. A good coach—a great coach—enables athletes to do more than they ever thought they could.

During my playing career, God providentially blessed me to play for great coaches: W. C. Treadway and Joel Sturdivant at Jones High School, Gene Stallings and Lloyd Taylor at Texas A&M, Don Shula and Bobby Boyd at the Baltimore Colts, John Madden and Bob Zeman at the Oakland Raiders, and Bum Phillips at the Houston Oilers.

Way before my playing career, even as a kid, I wanted to be a coach. I must have been trying to "coach" others, because I remember my dad telling me to stop telling my Little League baseball teammates how they should do things. Dad saw it as being a "know it all," (and it did look that way), but I really did want to coach others, and help them, especially in sports.

I'll be the first to say I'm not a great golfer (82'ish for 18 holes), but it drives me nuts to see guys whacking at the ball and doing it all wrong. If I know them well, I'll ask if I can show them one thing that I think would help. I've really helped some friends that way. And I do believe that a desire to coach is one of the many gifts from God.

This is probably why I felt so comfortable the first time, in 1988, I found myself sitting in a Bible study with men who were called to help their players reach their potential. I guess I felt like a "Bible coach" to coaches. I was convinced, in that first study, that God had surrounded me with some of the best leaders of men that Austin, Texas had to offer. It dawned on me that this could become the call of my lifetime, ministering to coaches through a unique Christian ministry that would be called Coaches Outreach.

A meeting like this is never dull. Always interesting. Many times these leaders will open their hearts and share tough experiences. Let me tell you, high school coaches are the salt of the earth. These men are called to be calm and composed during tense sporting events because so many young people depend on them. This kind of meeting, this circle of coaches, became a place where they could be open and honest about the pressures

15

of coaching. These men understood one another. They were called to influence and lead young lives. The term Band of Brothers comes to mind, and with Sisters included, of course!

HUSH UP AND LISTEN

One of these men, Coach Tommy Cox, became a good friend. I give Coach Cox credit for starting Coaches Outreach which only makes him shake his head in denial. He wrote the initial letter to all the coaches in Austin inviting them to the Texas High School Coaches Association offices for a Bible study. He was a respected coach who would later go on to be the athletic director in Austin over many of the schools represented around our circle. He was a tough-minded coach who expected nothing less than 100% effort from his players.

In one of our early studies, Coach Cox told us something that really struck me. He said that often his passion to see his players improve clouded his judgment. He shared how he was pushing a kid pretty hard. This kid was new to the game of football. Later, feeling badly about it, he felt the need to apologize for how he had addressed him in front of the whole team. At our study, Coach Cox asked us to pray for him since that day he would speak to the kid. Several coaches gathered around and prayed for him.

At the next weekly study, one of the coaches asked Coach Cox how it went with the player and the apology. He said he felt nervous when he called the kid into his office. But before

16

he could start, the young man broke the ice by apologizing to him! Tommy sat there, amazed, as the kid blurted out how sorry he was for screwing things up. He said the kid just kept going on and on about how he didn't have a dad in the house and that Coach Cox was like his dad. So the kid felt horrible—letting down his coach, this leader so important to his life.

Finally, Coach Cox interrupted him. He said, "It's okay. Just hush up and listen." That's Coach Cox, tough but tender. "I was praying last night and God convicted me. I had a bad day and in response, I picked on you. That was wrong. You work hard. And you're new at football. God impressed me that I needed to apologize to you. So, I'm sorry. Will you accept my apology?"

The kid said right away, "That's okay, Coach." Tommy said he got up, gave him a big hug and encouraged him. "Now, you get out there and just keep working as hard as you can. I'm proud of you." I glanced around the table. Several coaches were wiping their eyes. I heard a manly sniffle here and there. The truth is, everyone—including me—fought back tears. These men had the opportunity to daily inspire and change lives. They all understood that their "job" was not simply about wins and losses; they had been given a stewardship of young men's lives.

Coach Cox's response to that young player—including the apology, the hug, and the encouragement—demonstrates the caring support at the heart of Coaches Outreach. In every game, a few "big plays" appear to decide the outcome. And you see that same "big play" principle working out in our lives. God embeds certain moments in our brains, helping us to see, personally, the directives and opportunities he weaves into our lives.

What Coach Cox said that morning became a "big play" moment for me. I saw, in that one moment of honesty, the impact that a coach can have on young people. Our purpose in Coaches Outreach is to help coaches see how important they are, no matter what level or age they are called to impact.

Again, it's not about winning and losing. It's more than just training athletes to be good at what they do. It's about coaches loving those kids. And kids getting that, and loving their coaches in return. It's a relationship. A caring relationship, like a father to a son, knowing he is raising up the leaders of tomorrow's world. I see it as "biblical discipleship." And that involves shaping the next generation.

COACH PAUL

Paul the Apostle wrote many letters to New Testament churches, and you can pick up that sense of relationship in the tone of his writing. We know that Paul never married, but he had a fatherly approach, kind of like a coach's heart for the churches for which he had oversight. Listen to how he talks to Timothy, a young minister-in-the-making. Sure sounds like "Coach Paul" to me!

"You therefore, my son, be strong in the grace that is in Christ Jesus. The things which you have heard from me in the presence of many witnesses, entrust these to faithful people who will be able to teach others also. Suffer hardship with me, as a good soldier of Christ Jesus. No soldier in active service entangles himself in the affairs of everyday life, so that he may please the one who enlisted him" (2 Timothy 2:1-4 NASB).

We live by these verses at Coaches Outreach. We have similar verses displayed as metal plaques on the walls of our CO offices. It's a reminder. Like Paul and Timothy, we need to have "spiritual sons" in our lives. Every believer should have at least one person he or she mentors in the faith. Yes, it takes time. It takes planning, and probably going out of your way. But the results can be dynamic—and eternal. Once you get the hang of mentoring someone, then, with much prayer, go and find one more. And one more…watch your legacy grow!

USE ME TODAY

A friend of mine prays a simple prayer every morning. It's a powerful prayer, one that affects the person who prays it, and the people that person encounters. Here it is: "Lord, please use me today."

Told you it was simple. But I need to warn you. If you pray it—and if you mean it—then button your chin strap. That's an old football expression meaning, "You better get mentally ready for some intense action from an opponent!"

Let me put it this way. Many aspire, but few attain what the Lord expects of his children. "Go therefore and make disciples of all nations, baptizing them in the name of the Father and of the Son and of the Holy Spirit, teaching them to observe all that I commanded you. And behold, I am with you always, to the end of the age" (Matthew 28:19-20). This is the Great Commission. If you think about it, God has put Christian coaches in a position to see this happen in a dynamic way. Let me give you a clear example of a coach, who, at the professional level, understands his calling.

Coach Frank Reich is the former head coach of the Indianapolis Colts. Also a former pastor, Coach Reich speaks clearly about his faith in Jesus Christ. As a former Baltimore Colt myself, who came to the Colts as a new Christian, I remember not just winning the Super Bowl, but seeing firsthand the faith and life that many of the players modeled. The Colts back then had a great Bible study every Friday night taught by Captain Bill Lewis. This godly man lived 60 miles away in Annapolis, Maryland, and went the distance to bring us God's Word. It's possible he began his mornings praying, "Lord, please use me today."

I read a newspaper article recently about Coach Reich and his visit with the press after a big playoff win. It took me back to my days as a Colt. And reminded me that I was a big fan of Coach Tony Dungy who Coach Reich replaced at the Colts. Coach Dungy also shared his faith. He challenged his players to read through the Bible in one year with him. The article reported that Coach Reich, even in emotional and difficult moments, always came back to his faith. On one occasion, after a comeback victory in a playoff game, Coach Reich decided it was time to express his faith even more publicly.

Meeting with the press after a big game, some thirty years ago, he talked about a song that meant a lot to him. The song was "In Christ Alone," with the beautiful chorus, "In Christ alone, I place my trust, and find my glory in the power of the cross." Coach Reich went on to say, to everyone there, that his strength and hope was in Christ alone. And quoting another small verse from the song, he said about his Lord, "I seek no greater honor than just to know him more" (Brian Littrell lyrics.)

Coach Reich spoke from his heart, not knowing that another former Colt (me, 1969–1970) would read that article, say a little prayer thanking God for Coach Reich's boldness, and ask God to help me finish this book you hold in your hands (looks like my prayer was answered, doesn't it?). Coach Reich, who, in January 2023 became head coach for the Carolina Panthers, served as another great coach in my life at a time when I really needed a great coach's challenge. My heart was warmed and the article made me think back to some wonderful memories with the Baltimore Colts (Johnny Unitas, Tom Matte, Rick Volk, John Mackey, Bob Vogel, Lenny Lyles, Don Shinnick, etc.) and a bunch of other All-Pro players. Great memories.

THE REAL BATTLEGROUND

Let's go back to Coach Cox's conviction and apology with the player he picked on during practice. That moment put a seal on my heart of how important coaches are—especially Christian Coaches—in our society. And beyond that, in the world. These men deserve encouragement that only their Creator can fully give them. I still know, to this day, that God providentially took me through many unique experiences in sports and life to equip me to encourage these important men in our lives.

I'll tell you later about how Coaches Outreach got started, but soon after it became a full-time ministry, I met Coach Ken Hatfield. He played football at the University of Arkansas and became the head coach at Rice University. I called for an appointment with Coach Hatfield, and he invited me to come on by.

After describing my desire to encourage coaches with relevant Bible studies, Coach Hatfield said, "Tommy, I want to encourage you to stay right on track with this. And keep on working with high school coaches. I know that high school coaches look up to college and pro coaches, that's just the way it is. However, I look up to high school coaches, and here's why: these guys are in the real battleground of life and they need your support—especially making and keeping Jesus Christ central in all they do."

That was a perfect statement—spoken by an imperfect man—but used by a perfect God, at the perfect time! I carry Coach Hatfield's exhortation to this day. This is why Coaches Outreach focuses on junior and senior high school coaches, although college, professional, and Olympic coaches use our Bible studies as well. But very few get as close to influencing a young person's life the way a middle school or high school coach can.

If you know any coaches, thank them for their service, just like you would a police officer or any active or retired military veteran.

Playing professional sports, and working alongside all kinds of coaches, I've noticed something interesting. Did you know…

Great coaches are always successful when they leave coaching for another profession. I've seen it over and over. Why? Well, if you worked the hours they do, in a close relationship with thousands of kids—and the kids' parents—then any other job is easy for high school coaches. They have all the pressure that a college or pro coach has, yet college and pro coaches don't have to deal with raging hormones, parents who think their kid should be playing, classroom prep, low salaries for the long hours of work, and a dozen other things that high school coaches put up with. A former coach can tackle just about any job you can think of—and excel—due to the experiences of working in such an intense environment.

Christian coaches desire something more than just being great. Because coaching, from God's point of view, is more than just a job. It excels to a higher level. And calls us to a greater destiny. Coaching, you see, is a ministry.

CHAPTER 2
COACHING = MINISTRY

TREMENDOUS IMPACT

Everything I've learned about giving 100%, setting goals, sacrificing for a team, etc., all boils down to one powerful revelation: coaching is a ministry.

Coaches have a tremendous impact, not only on the lives of their players, but also on the non-sport students they meet and teach, as well as other teachers, school administrators, parents, and people in the community.

I have walked down a school hallway with a coach and watched as just about every kid looks over at the coach, hoping that the coach will notice them—if only with a smile.

I think God might be looking down on us with a smile, don't you? I mean, we think we have it all together. We think about our impressive plans, and how we get things done—our way. I've often thought that my experiences, my accomplishments, my victories, have been brought about by my plans. Then, it seemed as though God would step in and say, "Not so fast, Maxwell." He always had a better plan for me. And he took me through many years of various struggles to prepare me for what he wanted me to do.

I'm thankful for my pastor friend, Mitch Morrow, who helped me see God's direction after I told him about how I received my nickname, "Not So Fast," from the Oakland Raiders. After Mitch looked over several of my life stories, and saw all the 180 degree turns in different professions, he said, "*Not So Fast* is a good title for your book, Tommy." God used Mitch to not only jog my thinking about what this book should be, but to kick me off dead center, where book writers can get stuck. And as I said, Mitch set up the title, and it really fits. Let me tell you how that name came to be. As you'd expect, it's a funny story. Well, kinda funny.

Football teams have different teams-within-a-team. You have the kickoff team, kickoff return team, punt team, punt return team, etc. With the Raiders, I played on the punt return team as the up man (ten yards in front of the return man) and caught all the shorter, more difficult punts. I also played on the onside kickoff return team. I guess you could say that position was a somewhat honorable position because onside kicks are difficult to catch—spinning and bouncing as the ball comes your way. Yikes! They put the "good hands" players up front to receive the bouncing ball. Back in the '60s, the football was placed on the 40 yard line and had to be kicked at least ten yards to the receiving team.

Well, two weeks in a row our opponents kicked onside kicks, which are extremely rare in pro football. Guess who they both came to? Yep, lucky me. And, I bobbled both, but recovered them both each time. Whew! The next week on Friday review, they called out players to go to their special team positions, I trotted out to my "lucky" onside kick return position.

However, about ten feet away from me stood Coach John Madden. Then I heard my name. "Maxwell!" he called out, and—given the serious tone of his voice—I wasn't sure what was coming next. "We're putting Bob at your position," he said. A few things popped into my head, like "What'd ya say, Coach?" Or "Bob? Really?" or even "Wait a minute Coach, can we talk about this?" Those might have worked in junior high school—but in pro ball, it's not about your feelings, it's about performance. I had to swallow it. Embarrassed and trying to smile, I walked away, hiding a real punch to the gut. Adding insult to injury, a player hollered out, so everyone could hear it, "Not so fast, Maxwell!" I wanted to holler something back, but I didn't. But something good came out of it. "Not So Fast" stuck as a nickname. And because I had a nickname, I was— from that point onward—an official Oakland Raider.

The term *not so fast* may need a little explaining. It's an old expression you really don't hear much anymore, describing those who thought they were deserving of something—but didn't receive it. Like a raise. Or a pat on the back. People would say, "Hold it right there, buster." Or if someone cuts in line and a bystander calls out, "Not so fast, buddy!"

When I ran to my place in practice—thinking I had earned it and deserved it—Coach Madden called for someone else, better equipped, to step in and take it. "Not so fast" was like

"You're out, Maxwell, you bobbled the ball one too many times." That's why it hit me hard. Coach was saying, "Maxwell, you've been replaced." NSF again! So, the name stuck. And I deserved it. But it was memorable, that's for sure.

In fact, a Dallas friend of mine ran into Phil Villapiano (great Raider linebacker in the late '70s) and asked him if he played with me. He said, "Sure, I played with ol' Not So Fast." In fact, at a reunion in honor of the late George Blanda, former and present-day Raiders came together. One of the present-day players came up to me and said, "So, you're Not So Fast." I asked him how he knew my Raider nickname and he said, "We had a nickname party and you were voted as All-Time Best Nickname."

So now, I hope you can better understand where the crazy book title came from. As Pastor Mitch Morrow said, "Tommy, God has been saying, 'Not so fast, Maxwell' for a long time, to keep you on his track, and his timetable—not yours."

Sure enough, that nickname popped back up over and over again, as if the Lord knew how to get my attention. You'll see it several times in this book. Sometimes we'll just abbreviate it, NSF. When you see that, you'll know I'm in for a lesson, and a spurt of spiritual growth!

LOST OPPORTUNITY?

Many times God worked in spite of me to accomplish his purposes for Coaches Outreach. One time, I met with a coach in South Carolina to talk about the ministry. I was pumped to meet him at the stadium which was filled every Friday night with excitement. As I shared our ministry and showed him our latest Playbook, (what we call our Bible study), he kept checking his watch. That annoyed me—and made me uncomfortable. I asked him, politely, if he had somewhere to go. He said, "Just get to what you want, I'm very busy right now." The way he said it ticked me off, and, not so politely, I said, "I don't want anything. And what I have to show you, Coach, is way too important to rush through." I stood up, said "Nice meeting you," shook his hand, and left.

I was thinking about the lost opportunity and how I would be in trouble if the coach friend who set up the meeting heard from this coach. When my coach friend did call me, he said in no uncertain terms that the other coach thought I was a rude jerk. My intensity level (I should say anger) flared up as I told my coach friend that I thought the same thing about that coach! Then I heard some words I will never forget: "Tommy, after Coach Smith (false name) gave me his opinion of you, he asked me about the Bible study and I shared with him how much it had helped my coaching staff. He now wants to start a Coaches Outreach Bible study." I was floored! Never in my wildest imagination did I think this coach would be interested in our studies and ministry.

Lost opportunity? No, sir. I learned a big lesson from this encounter that would carry me through much of my leadership at Coaches Outreach. The big lesson, which I'd thought of as

29

just a theological concept—sovereignty, meaning God's control of all events—was a reality, not just to be acknowledged, but experienced. What I mean is, if the Lord wants something to happen, you cannot screw it up. It will happen. And he will use it for our good and his glory. Yep, God had shown me another Not So Fast moment. Jumping up to catch a pass is a good thing; jumping to conclusions is something else. Lesson learned. Don't judge a situation too quickly. God is always at work.

I believe God is still developing the ministry of Coaches Outreach, because I strongly believe that God desires for coaches to walk with him. It's a unique stewardship God has given them over the lives of their students and players. High school coaches often carry the most important influence outside the home, at a time when young lives are most easily influenced by online content, social media, negative peer pressure, etc.

The role of a coach is made even more stressful in marriage. Early on, Coaches Outreach began to provide marriage retreats in nice places for coaching couples at minimal cost (our ministry provides 75% of the cost). We have retreats in the summer before school starts so coaching couples can have good biblical teaching on marriage and the home before the grind begins. The coach's spouse can either be the biggest asset, teaming up with the coach's calling, or the greatest liability—growing bitter with the coach's long working hours. Most coach's spouses also work and may have the unenviable role of sitting in the stands and hearing everything called out about their husbands or wives.

During one particular game, a man showed up with a big sign that said, "FIRE THE COACH!" The more that coach's wife watched this idiot wave the sign, the angrier she became. Finally, she got up, went to the man's seat, grabbed his sign from him, busted it all up, and after a few choice words, went back and sat down. The crowd burst into a roar of applause. That, my friend, is a coach's wife!

For this reason, some coach's spouses prefer to sit in the press box where they can't hear all the hollering about their coach mates. Male spouses could just punch out any hollering male idiots, but I haven't heard of that. I do know that, many times, coaches can feel like they live in a fishbowl with critical people observing every move they make. If spouses are not fully on board with their coaches, it can spell disaster—and take away their passion for a sport they love to coach.

DAILY PASSION

The most important characteristic a coach can display is a passion for God and others, lived out in daily life. That passion, expressed as "Seek first the kingdom of God and his righteousness" (Matthew 6:33), can lead a person away from self-centeredness and into a God-centered life.

Some coaches only care about the title of "coach" without realizing how accountable they are to their Creator. Coaches who coach just for the money are called coaches who only "roll out the ball." Meaning, they just watch and herd kids without the gifted ability to inspire their players to become better.

And, for a Christian coach, whose faith is real and character is growing, he or she will have an eternal impact on young people.

In God's timing, he has raised up Coaches Outreach because our country needs God's coaches more now than ever. Coaches are more "hands on" in their relationships because of the intensity which comes with competition. The coach's walk counts more than just his words. Young people need examples more than they need lectures.

The average fan will never be happy without a championship every year. Yet, the majority of coaches will never experience a championship year. These fickle crowds result in the average coach moving every two to three years due to being fired. The best "character building coaches" coach for the kids, not the crowds. In high school, coaches can't go out and recruit the blue-chip athletes—they work with the kids God gives them. This is why Coaches Outreach is so vital, reminding coaches of their calling and never judging them by their win/loss record.

I visited with a coach at one of our marriage retreats. The speaker, standing before a room of coaches from all kinds of coaching situations, emphasized that if you love your athletes and students, then you are the real winner. The coach I was talking with said he had been coaching for twenty-one years and never won a championship. He was actually thinking about getting out of coaching. Then he told me, "The speaker tonight said that if you love your kids, then you're the real winner. Well,

I do love all the kids I coach. I spoke with my wife and I am going to stay in coaching. I feel like a winner now." Man, I loved hearing that.

But the truth is, as I've said, more and more coaches are quitting in alarming numbers and at an alarming rate. To make matters worse, the remaining coaches have to pick up the slack. That stretches them beyond their capacity. However, there's another problem, maybe even bigger than the first one.

Many of the newer, younger coaches don't have the maturity and wisdom that excellent coaching demands. So, with the relentless pace of a coach's life, they may feel unending frustration, which in turn may push them to consider quitting. And never coming back. As you read this, please pray for Coaches Outreach. Many great, older coaches are also leaving this great profession. Young coaches desperately need their modeling. I believe this ministry is vital— essential to giving coaches the strong encouragement they need. Because coaching is never easy. Never.

MORE THAN A LIVING

Career coaches put their heart and soul into each game. Each game matters. And each game leaves a lasting impression. You never get over certain losses—or wins. Coaching is draining. It can be hard on the family.

One of my high school coaches, Joel Sturdivant, always spoke about how our team had to wait in cold weather for a bus at Rice Stadium in Houston. Just after practice, the night before a big playoff game, Coach Sturdivant wanted to get us into the bus and head home to get ready for the next day. He didn't like us waiting out in the cold. I remember him saying in our visits together, "That late bus cost us the state championship!"

You may ask, "Cost us the championship?" Well, coaches feel good about good practices before big games. Coaches feel ready. Players feel ready. When you have a disorganized practice, with mistakes, coaches know that can make a difference in the game. Coaches live by the truth, "You play like you practice." Having players stand out in the cold, waiting on a bus that should have been there, can throw a wrench into the works. It can lead to a loss, and a big loss can stick with a coach for life, like injuries that never heal.

In our society today, it's hard to find role models you can trust as reliable examples to follow. Coaches who model a connection with God's attributes will reproduce God's attributes—wisdom, faithfulness, justice, mercy, unconditional love, and more. Coaches have great potential to make more than a living. They can make an eternal impact. They can introduce eternal life. We all need models of good coaching or mentoring no matter where we are in life. And we all coach someone.

My first motivation in writing this book was to show God's work in my life and how he led me to start a ministry to coaches. But as I wrote, I realized that my life story is not my own. I don't think for one second that any part of my life happened by accident or the result of clever planning. God has a plan for my life and yours. You can thank him for the good times and blame him for the bad times, but those who see that God is always good in his purposes—and bow to his purpose—are always thankful. In a good season; in a bad season. That thankfulness comes from getting hold of this solid, biblical principle: "And we know that God causes all things to work together for good to those who love God, to those who are called according to His purpose" (Romans 8:28 NASB).

It's God's very nature to be loving, kind, wise, just, and ultimately holy. God cannot deny who he is. He always shows his attributes to those who are thankful for him and submit to his Lordship. I want this for coaches.

God prepares each believer for a special ministry, and he will show his children their purpose. Even when I was going through tough situations—not seeing any kind of purpose—I went back to my nickname, a lifelong revelation and a constant reminder: "Not So Fast, Maxwell." The message: "Slow down, Tommy. Trust me. I've got it all under control." He was using everything—all the stories you're about to hear in these pages—to prepare me for Coaches Outreach. God always has a plan. Always.

GO HOME

One more story. For now, anyway. About 35 years ago, after playing golf one day, I was having lunch with a buddy and a friend of his joined us. After a lunch together, I said, "Well, it's time to go home to the family." No great testimony there.

However, twenty years later (let that sink in), that same young man came up to me and said, "I want to thank you." "What for?" I said. He went on to explain that when we had lunch back then, he was going through a divorce. My statement about going home to the family grabbed his heart. He and his wife called off the divorce and were now happily married and so thankful, for their kids' sake, that they were still together. God is not nearly as interested in our worldly success as he is in our heavenly significance. Awards or championships are nothing compared to his personal direction toward his personal purposes.

You might ask, "Will God work his personal, eternal purposes in my life?" I can answer that. If God can work in my life—with all the times I've bobbled the ball, and generally messed things up—God can and will work in your life too! I've come to believe that God can use anyone to do anything. At any time. There's no greater joy than seeing God work in the world through unspectacular people like you and me.

And friend, that's what the rest of my story is all about.

CHAPTER 3
GROWING UP

LITTLE TOM

Welcome to my childhood.

I was born Thomas Marshall Maxwell, in Houston, Texas in 1947 to Mary and Tom Maxwell. My grandmother, Bertha B. Grubb, called me Little Tom after my dad. My two sisters, Kay and Nancy, are eleven and seven years older than me. You could say I was the typical baby boomer born right after WWII.

About the age of 12, I realized that my dad was not that athletic. He was 40 years old when I was born, and sports were not a big part of his younger days. He graduated from Texas A&M (Class of '32) with an engineering degree, leading him to serve in the army during World War II as a colonel with the task of building bridges. Fun fact: the producers of the well-known Oscar-winning movie, *Bridge Over River Kwai*, interviewed Dad for his technical experience. When the war was over, he worked for the Amoco Oil Company for some 40-plus years.

My dad was an easygoing guy who could fix anything. He

never cussed or even raised his voice. He was a great model of faithfulness, dependability, and responsibility. He also liked to keep things simple which I see in my own life as well.

He may have been more athletic if sports had been a bigger thing in his day, but as it was, just playing catch, especially as I grew older, was not easy for him.

One time, when I was about twelve, my pitched ball bounced off his glove and knocked off his glasses. Right away, he hung up a big tarp, outlining the strike zone box on the tarp, and placed it the exact distance from our mock Pee Wee League pitcher's mound to the plate. Dad would sit by that tarp and roll the balls back to me time after time. He kept it simple, like I said.

As I think about it, I do remember him, every now and then, moving quickly and running fast. So, I probably got some speed from him.

I never saw my mom run. Ever. My mom's dad was a pretty big guy (6'4") judging by the few pictures I'd seen. He died in a car wreck just three months before I was born. Knowing my mom's brother, Uncle Jack, I can picture my granddad. Mom said he was a big teaser and loved telling stories. I was only around Uncle Jack a few times, but I remember him clearly: lots of fun, full of stories, and quick to tease (so that's where I got that from!). Neither Mom nor Dad would have imagined that I'd grow up to play pro ball, standing at 6'2" and weighing in at 200 pounds.

My engineer dad never taught me to fix things; I guess he realized that I'd rather be running, catching, and throwing. But his engineering did come into play on certain school day evenings. I clearly remember him sitting with me, trying to explain algebra. I listened—but never got it. He would explain it over and over, but he couldn't understand why it was so hard for me. After a while, I stopped asking him.

One thing Dad did bring into my life—something I've enjoyed all of my life—is the game of golf. One of his business friends gave him some clubs when he was 51 and I was 11. He quickly grew to love the game, and to this day I love golfing just as much as he did. It's a sports outlet for me.

Dad was a quiet guy, but I remember him speaking up at dinner one night saying, "Today I made a wise investment."

"Well, what was that?" my mom asked, rolling her eyes.

"A golf cart," he answered.

I'll never forget the look on my mother's face. "Well, my Lord," she sighed. And then just shook her head.

But I perked up. *Hmmm*, I thought, *that's really cool.* Soon after, I started learning to play golf. And I loved riding with Dad in the golf cart as much as playing the game. To this day, I still love it. Dad kept that same cart for the next 30-plus years of his golf habit. Yep, he could work on golf carts too!

He was always fixing things. Each leaky faucet, flickering light bulb, funny sound from under the hood—each became a challenge for him. I don't remember anything he couldn't fix! And I guess those things were small potatoes compared to rebuilding bombed-out bridges in the Philippines during WWII and starting from scratch by cutting down trees. That suited his engineering mentality and served the cause in a great way. Few could do what he was asked to do.

My mom, Mary Maxwell, was impressive in her own right. A very sharp lady. She was a part-time secretary, an excellent typist, and mastered shorthand so she could write down anything the boss would say—as fast he was saying it. A big plus.

Mom never went to college, but she read several books a week. She enjoyed temporary work, but her employers always begged her to stay on permanently. She must have felt proud about that because she told us about it on more than one occasion. Wink-wink. I remember her bridge-playing friends telling me, "Your mama is an unbelievable bridge player. She should go pro!" And in social situations, she was the star of the party— just the opposite of my introvert dad.

CLOSE CALLS

Throughout my young life, I always had a sense that God was watching over me. A sense that God's personal care was ever present—ever near. I learned to say the Lord's Prayer, probably from attending Sunday school at Garden Villas United Methodist Church. I said it every night before I went to sleep. Kind of a good luck charm, I guess. But I see now just how biblical and foundational that prayer was—and is—and how it sensitized me for the gospel, which came later in life during college.

I've had a couple of close calls in my growing up years. Those unforgettable moments have convinced me that God was there, watching over Tommy Maxwell.

In 1957, I was 10 years old. We lived on Sims Bayou in Houston, Texas. Since Houston was close to sea level, these bayous would take excess water to the coastline when heavy rains hit. My friends and I spent a lot of time playing along this bayou, shooting BB guns at the minnows in the bayou water.

I had several close encounters with water moccasin snakes. There were plenty of them. I stepped right on a big one and still don't understand why it didn't bite me. Well…yes, I do. I could move quickly—and God had a plan. If one had struck me, that would have been part of God's purpose also. You might rather say, "If God had allowed it to happen," if it makes you feel better. Either way, it was directed by God's perfect goodness and grace. Let me expand on this thought for a moment.

"And we know that for those who love God all things work together for good, for those who are called according to his purpose" (Romans 8:28). Hmmm. It does say, "his purpose," doesn't it? Let's face it, our Creator is either in complete control or he is not. He is in full control, in case you're wondering. The great God of heaven is never perplexed over what happens in his creation. Our merciful Father decrees all happenings: "The lot is cast into the lap, but its every decision is from the Lord" (Proverbs 16:33).

Most of us have thrown a coin up and pronounced, "heads or tails," and whatever side the coin landed on pointed to a particular directive or choice. God's will is always behind the flip of the coin (biblically called, "the casting of the lot").

41

Back to Sims Bayou. There's a particular train track I re-member—vividly—that ran about a quarter mile from my house. It crossed Sims Bayou on a train bridge (trestle) that was about 75 feet above the bayou. I was in the middle of that long bridge, by myself, all caught up in throwing rocks. Suddenly, I felt the tracks rumbling and looked behind me. A train was bar-reling down on me about 75 yards away!

I turned to run and my foot slipped down, caught between the cross ties. I was stuck! Panic set in as I desperately tried to wiggle my foot out. It wouldn't budge and the train kept-a-comin'! Finally, after yanking and struggling painfully, my bloody foot pulled free. Seconds felt like an eternity. I couldn't jump from the middle of the bridge since the narrow bayou—only three inches deep at the time—was 75 feet below!

I realized my only chance was to run toward the end of the bridge. I took off.

I guess the train engineer never saw me, because I don't remember hearing the sound of screeching train brakes. That meant—I quickly realized—the train was right on my tail.

The tracks were vibrating from the weight of it, and the heavy rumbling sound grew louder as it closed in.

I couldn't make it to the end of the bridge. So, my only hope was to jump down about 15 feet onto some large, jagged rocks stacked at the end of trestle. I took a running jump, and I remember seeing the train whiz by as I tumbled and crashed onto the sharply pointed rocks.

It's a wonder I didn't split my head wide open. I remember breaking my long fall with my legs and arms, landing in a

42

strange position.

I laid there, shaking, breathing hard, watching the train pass by overhead. Unless you've been close to a train, you don't realize how loud the thing is—roaring past you—and then how suddenly it's gone, and everything is quiet again.

When I stood up, I saw blood all over my t-shirt, and looked down at my blood-smeared ankle, missing a lot of skin. The adrenaline must have been flowing because I don't remember any pain until I started limping home.

I was a bloody mess. Somehow, I sneaked into our bathroom to clean up. I remember bruises and cuts all over my body, but I kept quiet so Mom wouldn't hear anything unusual.

When I walked casually into the room, she noticed—immediately. How could I hide the big knot on my head and a deep cut on my cheek? She inspected it, then asked how it happened.

Well, I lied to her and said I got hurt playing a pickup football game. I didn't want to have to explain to my parents (or a doctor) what had happened. And I never did. I thought about that train encounter for months. Even now, the traumatic scene sticks in my mind. I still find myself saying, often, "God had a purpose."

God gave me speed, not just to run fast, but to tell me when to jump and land me bloody and bruised—but alive!—on those dangerous rocks. His running gift ultimately led to a high school city championship, a college scholarship, a Cotton Bowl victory team, and a Super Bowl victory game. But no more throwing rocks from train trestles.

FIRED UP

I do know this about myself. God created me to need excitement.

I grew up loving sports. I like to be around people fired up about sports or at least about something. I find myself bored with the mundane and always looking for a "scoring" moment.

I can't help it. I bore easily.

Since I was 10 or 11 years old, all my decisions have been made in an average 5 second time frame. That's the length of the average football play, and one team psychologist told me that my life reflected a built-in need for stimulation—which I already knew.

Early in life, I loved both baseball (especially batting) and football because of the quick decisions and stimulation involved. To be honest, my need for stimulation, along with my ADD, has made it difficult to write a book. To keep up with it. No more difficult than jumping off that bayou bridge, but I'm trusting that God's purposes will be honored in this leap as well.

In my younger days, organized sports didn't even start until kids reached about 10 years old, and they usually meant involvement with Little League baseball. So, most sports back then were pickup games in the neighborhood. Someone's front yard or an empty lot down the street would serve as our football or baseball field. I loved baseball so much that I'd have my uniform on hours before we left for a game. I was suited up, mitt in hand, and couldn't wait to get there.

In those first baseball years, I got good at stealing bases. I learned that as soon as the pitcher started his windup, I could take off for the next base. Yep, I'd be on third base after the pitcher's first two windup motions.

Sometimes I'd steal home as soon as the catcher threw the ball back to the pitcher. That was exciting! Of course, stealing bases became more challenging, but I became faster and loved stealing all the way up through Pony League baseball, geared for young people ages 13 and 14.

FIRST FOOTBALL GAME

In 1958, I turned 11 and had my first organized football game. My folks took me to the field. I found my way to the dressing room. Inside, everyone was changing clothes for the game, putting on their uniforms. But, of course, I had no idea how to do it. It wasn't like clothes I'd ever worn before. I remember my embarrassment. I was so uncomfortable in that dressing room. Someone must have helped me, I'm sure of that. And finally, there I was, out on the field, ready to go.

As the game progressed, the coach called me to go in for Bobby at defensive tackle. "What's a defensive tackle?" I asked. "Go in and tell Bobby to come out," the coach said. I was, shall we say, guided into my position by other players and I remember seeing this big offensive lineman, directly in front of me, almost twice my size. All I remember is that I did not like playing that tackle position. It was no fun and definitely not exciting.

BABY OILERS

I only played that one game before I was introduced to our church football team. I was 13 or 14 by then, in 1960–61. The church team needed a quarterback. I remembered that position from my neighborhood football games. I could throw and run so I got the job as quarterback. It was great. I was in on every play and loved it. What a fun year!

We had a good coach, Ted Scruggs, who had played football for Rice University. His wife, Elaine, was actually one of my mom's bridge partners. Coach Scruggs played a big part in my young football days, not only as my coach, but also by introducing me to a renegade new team in Houston called the KILT Baby Oilers.

KILT was a popular new radio station in Houston famous for their sports orientation. In the early 1960s, they started announcing tryouts for a new Pop Warner-like team named the KILT (like a Scottish kilt) Baby Oilers, geared to 13- and 14-year-olds. The KILT radio station sponsored the team and so did the Houston Oilers pro football team. The Oilers later moved to Tennessee and became the Tennessee Titans. Houston, years later, acquired a new football franchise, the Houston Texans. Back to the Babies.

Well, I was playing in my yard one Saturday when Mr.

Scruggs came to the house with a carload of boys including his son, Ted Jr. Mr. Scruggs went in and talked to my parents about this new team and before I knew it, I was on my way to try out for the KILT Baby Oilers.

The tryout was next to Jeppesen Stadium in Houston where the University of Houston, the Houston Oilers, and different Houston high schools would play their games. It was within a few weeks of football season and Jeppesen stadium had very little grass. Keep in mind, no artificial turf back then. This was the real thing, real grass which wasn't always in the best condition for football games. I remember losing a football shoe in the mud on that field while running for a touchdown. Oh, did I mention that Houston is known for lots of rain?

There had to be at least 300–400 kids trying out for this new team that had been advertised on KILT radio. They put us through all kinds of time trials, running through different challenge courses. It was fun and exciting.

But the truth was, I really didn't want to be part of the Baby Oilers because I was set up to play quarterback for Hartman Junior High School. But then, something interesting happened after the time trials that day. They brought out the KILT Baby Oilers uniforms.

Whoa! That did it. For me, and many of the guys, there was an immediate attitude change. These were silky-like uniforms with two—count 'em, two—sharp-looking jerseys. One black with red numbers and the other, red with black numbers. The stretch pants—really cool!—had a black and red stripe on the side of the pants. Hey, come on, these were like college or pro football uniforms! We all stood there and looked at each other. Each of us was thinking the same thing. We had to get picked for this team!

With the trial course over, it was time to go to the stands while they called out 33 names. Well...they picked me! And the uniform was my first thought! I'm not sure which of my friends made it, but some really good ball players became part of this little Baby Oilers team which I believe competed as a team for just two more years, going against other junior high teams.

Two players on that Baby Oiler team became my teammates at Texas A&M: Jack Whitmore and Larry Stegent. Both went on to become good college players.

Larry was three-times ALL-SWC (Southwest Conference) for Texas A&M and drafted in the first round by the St. Louis Cardinals pro football team. Sadly, he tore his knee up in training camp. Larry was a great runner with great hands. I know he would have been an outstanding pro running back, but when his injured knee became re-injured, his football career was over. However, and this happens a lot, Larry became a very success-ful insurance agent. As I said, and I've seen it many times across my experience: great players carry success into whatever they decide to do.

One day, the Baby Oiler coach, Zane Chastain, also a Houston sportswriter, asked the 33 picked players sitting in the stands, "Who plays on the line?" Only a few hands went up. Speed and agility determined how we were assigned positions. I stayed in the back field. But fortunately—we were all fast!

We won 29 out of the 30 games we played that first year.

We practiced once a week and played twice a week against any junior high school in Houston or close by. What a blast! We turned into a celebrity team. Our winning record became regular news in the Houston papers and on KILT radio.

At one of the Houston Oiler home games, the Baby Oilers were divided up and played at halftime. Don't let that slip past you—we played at halftime! Wow! I'll never forget lining up on the sidelines after our halftime performance and shaking hands with my heroes like George Blanda, Charlie Tolar (the human cannonball), and Charlie Hennigan. I went to most of the Oiler home games since Baby Oilers could attend free. They gave each player a special sport coat with a Baby Oiler patch on the pocket. I was always looking for someone to take me to every home game. Somehow, I always found a way there and I never missed one.

During that first year, the Baby Oilers traveled to California and played a top Pop Warner team. We beat them soundly. Then, my second year with the Baby Oilers, we played a top team in the Washington, D.C. area. Two of us players stayed in an opposing player's home with his crazy dad. He accused our players of lying at the weigh-in since their team had weight limits. His son and the other team players were all larger players than us, so his accusation was ridiculous. But very awkward. Again, in God's providence, I had an uncle who lived in the D.C. area. I called him and said I was half scared of this man. Uncle Ernie came and picked us up and we stayed with him. And, to round things out, we also beat the D.C. team! We beat them with speed—not size. Our players were a lot smaller—

but we still won. That was sweet.

While with the Baby Oilers, we also had the opportunity to play against my school, Hartman Junior High. Let me give you a little background on that game. Since I was supposed to be the new quarterback for my junior high, the football coaches were not too happy with me when I joined the Baby Oilers. In fact, I remember how they teased me and made me feel like a traitor. At some point my parents had a little powwow with the head coach and things became better after that.

When the Baby Oilers played against Hartman Junior High, I made a bet with the Hartman head coach that whoever won the game could give a pop to the loser. We won! The time came to give the coach a pop with his paddle. Well, let's just say it didn't quite work out. The coach positioned himself so close to the wall that I couldn't get a good swing. That was disappointing, but the greater outcome is knowing that the Hartman coach went on to be a really good encourager. As someone has said, "Finish well."

HERE TO HELP

During this time, I went with my parents to their friend's home for dinner. My parents told me they had a son with muscular dystrophy. My folks encouraged me, "Just play with him and be his friend." I did.

And later, I took him to the movies. He struggled walking, and one time, with a sudden spasm, he pitched into a person's lap. I didn't know how to respond, except to help him up and get him carefully to our seats. From there, we enjoyed the movie.

Through this experience, my folks taught me a great lesson. Every time I see someone with a disability, I realize we are here to help people. Sometimes I'll see someone, like my friend, and just go over there and talk to them. I'm thankful for that sense of freedom, that confidence, to feel comfortable with a disabled person. It's true. We're here to help.

SMOKEY

I don't remember asking for a horse.

I was a city kid in a small house on a bayou in Houston. People really didn't have horses in those neighborhoods. Dogs and cats maybe. Guinea pigs or hamsters in cages. But not horses! We didn't have a pasture or wide spaces for a horse— like I said, it was just a small neighborhood.

Anyway, for Christmas, when I was 12, my parents gave me a horse. I remember my dad, the fixer, putting up a fence behind our house. We had about a half acre since part of the backyard was on a bayou. I remember the fence going up and Dad saying that the city might make him take it down, but they never did.

But Dad wasn't done. He also built a small barn for the horse, the hay, and the horse feed. So, there I was, a city kid in a city neighborhood with a horse.

The horse's name was Smokey and he was downright mean. We did not like each other. He would walk around with me on his back, but if I ever tried to run him, he would start bucking. I tried to hold on, but…up and off! Into the air and down I went. Some of those landings on asphalt roads hurt! And I am sure—positively sure—I could hear that mean-hearted horse laughing as he threw his head up and down, while I laid there on the ground, flat out, groaning. And, well, to be honest, I did have a cussing problem back then, so I'm sure that old Smokey never heard his real name. I gave him some ugly new ones, if you know what I mean. But pain can bring out the worst in a man, even if that man is only 12.

One day, Smokey trotted straight toward some low tree branches. I pulled back on the reins—hard—but it didn't work. He took me right under those branches and knocked me off.

Another time, I went up to him inside his fence and tried to give him a carrot. He reared up on his hind legs and tried to come down on me. I took off for the barbed wire fence and remember leaping over it with that dang horse right behind me. Again, good thing I could run! But my leg didn't quite make it over and the barbed wire put a nice slice on my calf. Again, I thanked God, whom I didn't really know personally at the time, for getting me over that fence.

They stitched me up and followed it with a tetanus shot. I was still healing up after being chased by the train, and now this stupid horse! That did it. I told my folks I was going to kill that horse. Well, that didn't happen, but I was one happy camper when they sold him. Good riddance, Smokey.

But that's not the end of the horse story.

My folks found another horse. She was half Morgan and half Quarter horse. Her name was Minny, and she was nice and gentle. Repeat, nice and gentle. I rode Minny all over southeast Houston. I had a friend, Jimmy Works, who had a horse, too, and we would take off early on Saturday mornings. We crossed major highways (my folks never knew) and had a blast watching the planes land at Hobby Airport, Houston's main airport at the time.

We would lay down a blanket, pull out our PB&J sandwiches, and watch the big passenger planes fly over our heads, coming in for a landing. They seemed just a few feet away. They sounded that close, too! I'm sure the men in the control tower saw us, but they never ran us off. I'm not sure it was the smartest or safest place to be, especially with horses, but it all worked out and we did enjoy our freedom. Saturdays were ours! "Be home by dark" was the only order I ever heard. But hunger would always get me back on time, if not before.

UNBELIEVABLE CATCH, TOMMY!

While growing up in Houston, God put another coach in my life: Dudley Works. He was the dad of my friend Jimmy Works. Since my dad was not the greatest thrower or catcher of a baseball or a football, I hooked up with Coach Works, who coached my first Little League baseball team. I knew that Mr.

53

Works came home about 5:30 p.m. every weekday and was always home on the weekends. Guess who "showed up" at 5:30 p.m. and on the weekends? You got it. I loved the way Mr. Works could throw the baseball or football where I had to run and dive to catch it. I would do that as long as he would throw it. I absolutely loved it.

And I know Mr. Works loved watching me bust my butt to make the catch. I can still hear him saying, "Unbelievable catch, Tommy!" I credit God and Mr. Works for any speed and desire to catch a ball. I just wish I would have tried to contact him, to thank him, and not let the years go by. Mr. Works was the right coach for the right time in my life. Maybe my friend, Jimmy, will find this little book...and smile.

It just shows that you don't need to be a professional coach to impact a neighborhood kid. God used Mr. Works to impact me and tie into God's plan for me to have a ministry to coaches. I hope Mr. Works knew Christ as his personal Savior so I will see him in heaven. If he is there now, he has received rewards for every kid he impacted. Add to that every kid influenced by a coach who was encouraged by the ministry of Coaches Outreach. And, that would be, at least, thousands and thousands of kids!

CHAPTER 4

NEW SCHOOLS, NEW COACHES

PICK ME! PICK ME!

I felt at home at Garden Villas Elementary School. I attended there from 1954 to 1957. I remember the desks, the classrooms, my friends. And it wasn't that far from our house.

But then came Hartman Junior High School, 1957 to 1960, a larger, fairly new school. And I had become a different person. By this time, I was aware of girls. And they scared me.

I know that because, at Hartman, a friend and I both had a crush on the same girl. I say girl, when really, she was the Spanish teacher. But she was cute, and we were always competing for her attention. Sometimes she asked a question or looked around for volunteers to translate a sentence into Spanish. Whether or not we even knew the answer, we shot our hands into the air, wildly waving them around. I'm sure we had "Pick me!" written all over our smiling faces. My friend sat across the room from me, so we were always eyeing each other, hoping the other might forget to raise his hand. It was a fierce competition. No one else dared to enter. I remember some guy in front of me raising his hand and I immediately told him to put it down—or else! Still, when all was said and done, I guess my buddy and I learned a lot of Spanish.

After Hartman, I attended Jesse Jones High School from 1960 to 1965. Jones was an even newer, more modern school. There was the smell of fresh paint on the walls and the feel of new desks and lockers. I was so ready for sports, but of course, I had to take classes, too.

I remember this one chemistry teacher. One day in class— out of the blue—he began talking about eternal things. It was really kind of intense, like getting right to the heart of the Gospel. He had my full attention. He probably had the attention of everyone in the room. Best as I can remember, he said something like this:

"If you believe that Jesus died on the cross in your place, taking upon himself God's judgment, making you perfect before God—and this is not true—you have lost nothing.

"But if you don't believe that Jesus died on the cross in your place—and it is true—you are forever alone and condemned to a place called hell. You have lost everything."

Some years later, after my junior year at Texas A&M, I traveled to England, a stop on my way to Italy, where my sister's husband served in Naval Intelligence. The trip was a gift from my parents, and I was supposed to travel with a friend, but it didn't work out, so I went there alone. Walking through Hyde Park, I heard a loud, angry voice. I turned to see a guy standing on a platform, a wild Scottish atheist, with a red beard, shouting out, "There is no God!" It was the first time I'd come across anything like that.

This guy was acting like he knew it all, and it bothered me. Not having a Bible, or really knowing the Bible, I went up to this wild man and calmly repeated what the chemistry professor had said. It didn't help—the guy got in my face and shouted all the more. So, I went on my way.

But I think that crazy guy may have planted a seed in me, a desire to really know the Bible, and have a sound, biblical answer, as Peter said, "…always being prepared to make a defense to anyone who asks you for a reason for the hope that is in you; yet do it with gentleness and respect" (I Peter 3:15).

TREADWAY OR THE HIGHWAY

I dove headfirst into high school sports. Somehow I got involved in football, baseball, basketball, and swimming! That may be why I remember falling asleep trying to do homework at night. And why, across all my high school years, I had only one steady girlfriend, but only for a few months. The problem was, she wanted me to call her every night and come to school early to spend time with her, and, well, with my sports schedule, I just couldn't do it. I had to say goodbye. I won't say I left her for athletics, but you can draw your own conclusion. If Janice, my future wife, had been at Jones instead of Brady High School, it would have been a different story for sure.

Sports was everything. Finishing 9th grade playing with the Baby Oilers, I was anxious for my next big sports adventure: high school football. My head coach was W.C. Treadway. We referred to him as "Treadway or the Highway." He was a tough, motivating coach, who played football for Rice University. He made Coach Gene Stallings at Texas A&M look like a softy (although my A&M teammates will never believe that!).

This next thing is strange, I guess, but true: once in high school, and playing football, I discovered that band people were bad people. Keep reading before you judge me. Only later did I discover that people who were part of a high school band could actually be nice, talented, and, by and large, successful people. Okay, let me explain.

The band practiced long hours just like the football team. Some band members in other schools even played football and marched in the band at halftime—wearing their football uniform! Yet, whenever a player missed a tackle or a block during practice, Coach Treadway would point to the practicing band and say, "Why don't you just go over there and join the band?" We were all thinking the same thing: Oooh, band is bad. Not sure why, they're just bad. Or at least inferior. It's the place you did not want to go. So, for the coach, and as a result, in my football thinking, those were bad people. Made up of kids banished from football practice, I guessed. Don't worry, I figured it out finally and changed my mind. That was just Treadway… being Treadway.

NO-NONSENSE STURDIVANT

Coach Sturdivant was my football position coach and track coach at Jones High School. He was a no-nonsense coach but had an easy smile. Some years back, we reconnected, and I had some good visits with him. I'd forgotten how much I liked him and how much he influenced my life. We stayed in contact for many years.

He was an encourager. He was that personal model I could look to when we started up the Coaches Outreach ministry. He really pushed me in track and took a personal interest in me. He went on to be the beloved principal of Reagan High School in Houston.

Here's an example of Sturdivant-style encouragement. I was a late bloomer. And I'd lost some speed when I hit a growing streak, shooting up three inches in my sophomore year and four inches total in high school. I asked Coach Sturdivant, in my senior year, "Coach, what's wrong with me? Guys I could outrun last year are beating me now." He smiled and said, "Tommy boy, you'll be okay. Your legs just need to catch up to your height. Hang in there."

One time, he pulled me aside to have a talk. He told me they were going to hold me back from playing varsity my junior year. That was not what I wanted to hear, as you can imagine! But I knew I could trust him. Even though friends were moving up to varsity, I accepted my junior varsity status.

It turned out that our junior varsity team that year was the best in Houston! Many of those players—me included—moved up to varsity my senior year. And, we won the city champion-ship!

Was God in that? You can say to me all day, "Tommy, things just happen. You were lucky." However, when you per-sonally know and serve the sovereign God of the universe, statements like that just don't hold up. They reveal a kind of weak, worldly optimism, and it makes me feel sorry for people who don't know the Lord in a personal way.

I remember Coach Sturdivant always bringing up the fact that Jones High School should have been state champions my senior year. As I mentioned before, he blamed it on a bus. A bus that was late picking up our team after practice at Rice Uni-versity's stadium, where we prepped for our regional playoff against Galena Park the next night. Coach would say, "You guys stood outside in the wet, cold air and waited around—for way too long. It took our edge off, dang it." Coach remembered that game all too clearly, describing plays that went wrong.

One funny play (not so funny then) happened when Galena Park's "Chunkin' Charlie" Riggs (whom I later played with at A&M) threw a deep pass to Gilbert Ash. Van Brown (our great QB) and I were covering Gilbert (we played both ways back then). Ash fell down, Van and I bobbled the ball back and forth to each other a couple of times, and then the ball just tumbled into Ash's hands—while he was laying on the ground—in the end zone! Van and I just stood there in amazement. I'll never forget Ash jumping up, whooping and hollering. That TD ended a great season, but we were still city champs—a big deal since we competed against the largest schools in a city the size

60

of Houston.

That same year I led the city in TDs, with a total of 11 touchdowns. I'll never forget walking out and looking at a big sign in our front yard that said, "MR TD LIVES HERE." Thank you, Jones High School Booster Club!

And I'll never forget my dad, who faithfully attended my games throughout high school and college. A newspaper article picked up on this and said: "Mr. Maxwell, with Pan American Petroleum, has watched young Tommy play football in organized games for 12 years." Then Dad was quoted as saying, "I never missed a game in high school or at A&M. We're a closely knit family."

SPLASH

Another big part of my youth was competitive swimming. I took lessons from Emil Mamaliga who went on to be the strength coach while I played at Texas A&M. I started going to swim meets in and around Houston in the summers of my younger teen years. It became a real love and the long practice hours kept me out of trouble. My best stroke was the butterfly. Competitive swimming was big in Houston and there were quite a few swim teams. I remember the Dad's Club and my team, the Tropicana Swim Club.

In high school, I would leave football practice to be part of the swim team. The swim coach somehow convinced the football coach, Coach Treadway, to let me leave practice for maybe a half an hour when we had a swim meet at school. Most of the big high schools in Houston had pools. So, I would leave football practice, go in and take off my pads, put on my swimsuit, and either do an individual swim or swim the butterfly stroke on our medley relay team. I loved that. It was refreshing to leave the field and splash into the water. Then, it was back on with the pads and back to the football field! I think I only did that my sophomore year.

I still love swimming. It's a lifetime sport like golf. Knees and joints all start aching as you become older, so running is pretty much out of the picture. And swimming is great exercise anyway.

I had grown up dreaming of being an Olympic swimmer. But again, I grew up in Texas. And here in Texas, if you can run fast and catch a football, you end up on the field. Unlike swimming, there are no little ropes to keep you from the other athletes, so lots of people—big people—come running after you, wanting to take you down!

So, I mentioned the somewhat steady girlfriend I had for a few months at Jones High. And like I said, if it had been Janice, I would have definitely called her every night and showed up early at school to spend time with her. But I didn't meet Janice until college. I'll let her tell you her story, in her own words. I want you to get to know Janice Maxwell.

TALLER THAN THE BOYS

From Janice Maxwell

I grew up in the small, vibrant town of Brady, Texas, a town of 6,000 people at that time. Brady likes to call itself "The Heart of Texas" because it's the city closest to the geographic center of the state.

Living in Brady was like being in the TV show *Father Knows Best*. We lived in a cozy little two-bedroom, one-bathroom house, perfect for my mom, my dad, me, and my sister, Joan, three years younger than me.

Joan and I both took piano lessons. I didn't think I was that good, but Joan could really play. Our dad, Breck Breckenridge, my mom, Mildred, and our paternal grandparents faithfully attended First Baptist Church of Brady. We walked to church, and of course, us kids rode bikes all over town. I spent a lot of time at my grandparents' ranch, loving horses, cattle, and sheep. Really, my heart was in the country, and—at that point anyway—I hoped to marry a rancher.

But from the time I was a little girl, I loved twirling. At a young age, I could roll the baton over my arms, toss it up— spinning—and catch it, no problem. So, years later, I went on to be a majorette at Baylor University.

But in my elementary years, I enjoyed playing catch with guys in the neighborhood. I could easily keep up with them. I was tall for my age—taller than most of the boys—and was good at baseball and roller skating.

Going to Brady High School was a big change. For the first

63

time, the boys were taller than me! My sophomore year I came home to tell my mother the boys were taller. It was that kind of family. You shared the ups, the downs, and everything in-between.

I got involved in student council and served as editor of the school yearbook staff. Of course, I was part of the high school band which won a sweepstakes competition, both as a symphonic band and a marching band. There I was, a twirler, high-stepping it in front of the band, five or six of us, with the drum major leading the way. I loved being part of it all.

And whatever Tommy might have been told about high school bands, my involvement as a twirler, later in college, must have helped to change his mind!

My daddy went to all the football games. And since our house was two blocks from the high school, if we ever did miss a game, we could still feel the excitement, hearing the sound of the crowd and seeing the glow of the Friday night lights.

What a wholesome upbringing. And a simpler time. And even though we didn't have internet or social media, if you did do something wrong, your parents probably already knew about it before you came home!

In fact, I really didn't want to leave home to go to college. I remember sitting in my Daddy's lap, crying. But he wouldn't budge. He must have said it several times. "You have to go to college. You have to." What could I do?

So, I picked a school, North Texas State University (now known as University of North Texas), since a lot of my friends were going there. But then I heard other friends talking about

Baylor. Well, on the way to North Texas, we went through Waco and toured Baylor. It struck me as a beautiful campus. And I thought something unusual at that point. I thought, *this is a place where I could get closer to the Lord.* God was working on me.

Next day, we went to North Texas. It's funny, but I didn't like the place. I mean, I really didn't like it. Some of the people were rude. And to be honest, the campus just wasn't as beautiful as Baylor. We knew Baylor was expensive, but my grandfather, who worked hard all his life, loaned money to my parents to help meet the expenses. And so there I was, where I needed to be—at Baylor University. I'm getting ahead of Tommy's story now, but at Baylor the Lord began to prepare my heart for things to come.

Specifically, in my junior year there, the Lord was making my faith stronger and more central to my life. Around that time, I decided that whoever I married would have to be a Christian. But I never steadily dated anybody.

Then, in the fall of my junior year, and well into senior hours, I thought, I haven't met a single guy that I could trust with my life. Not one that I would think about marrying. So, I backed off from all dating. I just stopped. I wanted to be the Lord's person. And I wanted the person I would date, and marry, to have God as the center of his life.

It's funny how putting God first makes all the other things fall into place. Makes me think of Matthew 6:33, "But seek first the kingdom of God and his righteousness, and all these things will be added to you."

65

NOT SO FAST

What happened then?

November the 5th of that year, I met Tommy Maxwell.

And by Christmas, I was head over heels.

CHAPTER 5
A&M & STALLINGS

TORN BETWEEN SCHOOLS

After high school football, life became a journey of decisions called the college "recruiting trail."

I was recruited by just about every school in the old Southwest Conference. That included teams like Baylor, SMU, TCU, Arkansas, Texas Tech, Rice, Texas, and Texas A&M. All the colleges I visited put on their best front. It made me want to go to the last school I just visited. That made the decision process difficult. Fun, but difficult.

My A&M alumni contact in Houston was Lloyd Hale, a former center for Texas A&M under Bear Bryant. I really liked Lloyd and his wife, Joan, but I didn't want to play for Texas A&M since they'd been losing a lot of football games—for a long time. However, I felt a loyalty to A&M because my dad went there. But I verbally committed to Southern Methodist University after my visit there. Why? An 18-year-old kid used this reasoning: "Heck, I was a Methodist and they got me a cute date to a basketball game!" Reason enough, right? However, I liked Lloyd so much (I worked for him one offseason while I was in pro ball), that, just for Lloyd, I visited A&M the weekend before signing day.

As I trudged along the recruiting trail, I found myself torn between several schools.

I really liked the TCU coach who recruited me, and Arkansas was beautiful. At Arkansas, football players showed us around the school—but we never stopped for lunch. We kept asking, "What about lunch?" They kept reminding us to be patient, but hunger and patience don't go together with teenage guys. On and on we went. "When are we going to get there?" was all they heard while driving us to—can you believe it?— dinner!

Finally—after sundown—we arrived at a restaurant in the middle of the Arkansas hills. But there was a long line waiting to get in! Stomachs grumbled. Voices griped. As they say, you could cut the tension with a knife.

One of the Arkansas players hosting us went to the head of the line and into the restaurant. He came back and said, "Follow me." We went right in!

And before we recruits could say "Sooo-ee pig!" we were feasting on a 24-ounce steak piled high with french fries. Now I recognized their strategy! And it worked! Thanks to a 24-ounce steak! Whoever said the way to a man's heart (and head) is through his stomach—I guess they were right.

I considered my options: Cute date, SMU? Nope. Friendly coach, TCU? Nope. I chose a steak! Arkansas sounded—or tasted—really good! And though I didn't have my future title yet, "Not So Fast Maxwell," I was jumping to conclusions like a pro.

But after thinking it through, and still feeling torn between opportunities, and though not very excited about A&M (no steak I guess), I felt I should visit Texas A&M, if only for my dad and Lloyd Hale.

FACE TO FACE WITH STALLINGS

While on that recruiting trail, I met Glenn Smith, the quarterback for Waltrip High School in Houston. We hit it off, visiting the same colleges at the same time. We'd both verbally committed to SMU and made a pact with each other to go there. But we were at Texas A&M the same weekend, both sitting in the lobby of Coach Gene Stallings' office.

Just before I went in to visit with the coach, Glenn said, "Tommy, remember our pact. I'll be throwing you the ball at SMU, right?" "You bet," I said, and I went into the appointment.

Coach Stallings, the new head coach for A&M, shook my hand. He oozed with confidence and had a direct, no-nonsense way about him. I liked that.

He welcomed me to a chair and I sat down. Then he pulled up a chair—right in front of me. He looked at me intently. "Tommy, didn't yore daddy (Texan for "your" daddy) attend here at A&M?" "Yes sir," I responded.

"I bet yore daddy would sure like to see this program get

69

turned around, wouldn't he?" I felt like my foot was once again caught in the train track, feeling the rumble of the train bearing down on me. "Yes sir," I said.

Coach Stallings continued. "Did you know that I played football here at A&M under Coach Bear Bryant?" "Yes sir," I said again.

"Well, since yore Daddy went to A&M, and he'd love to see this program turned around, and since they hired me to turn things around, we need some ball players to help us do just that. You will come here and help us…won't you Tommy?"

Uh oh, this foot ain't coming out. He had me. "Yes sir," I heard myself say, and sealed it (Texas style) with a big handshake.

As I turned and approached the door, a cold thought shivered through me. I knew who would be sitting just outside it— my SMU buddy, Glenn. Ohhh, my gosh. And I had just shaken hands with Coach Stallings!

Well, I walked into the waiting room. Glenn looked at me, giving me a wink and a thumbs-up. It was like a "I know you're still with me," thumbs-up. He passed me and walked toward Coach Stallings' office. Sorry to say, I'm not sure how that played out, but I do remember that I hung my head and tried not to make eye contact as I passed.

That was the first major decision I had ever made on my own. It was tough.

As I said, I'd always been loyal to A&M since my dad went there, but since they didn't win many games back then, in the early 1960's, I still felt uneasy. Did I do the right thing? Did I buckle under Coach Stallings' pressure?

I talked to Dad about it, and though he liked the idea of me going to A&M, he and Mom said it was my decision. If they had a preference, they hid it well.

I remember going out to dinner with my parents and their friends just two days before the official signing date. Then— with no hesitation and definitely no forethought—I stood up from the table. Of course, they all looked at me. My mom, sensing I'd made up my mind, said, "Well, Tommy, where are you going to go?" I responded, "I'm going to call Lloyd Hale and tell him I am signing with A&M." They looked at me and smiled. Next thing I remember, I was on the phone with Lloyd.

From 1965 to 1969, I would be an Aggie at Texas A&M. Some of the very best years of my life.

But before I ever joined the Raiders and got my NSF nickname, I was already modeling a Not So Fast way of doing things. Sometimes I made snap decisions, while other times I held back, reacting with wisdom and boldness. And though I hadn't yet made a decision for Christ, God was (and is) sovereign over all things. All things. He is Creator, First Cause, and Master of the Universe. So, did the God of Creation stand me up and cause me to call Lloyd? Yes, he did. And I'm so grateful.

AGGIELAND DAYS

I remember our first freshman game against TCU.

Back then you were required to play on a freshman team.

So, freshmen played the freshmen from other colleges. Texas Christian University was our first game and TCU had recruited Norm Bulaich and Ross Montgomery, the two best high school running backs in Texas. Together they ran up a total of about 500 yards in that game. As we left Kyle Field, Coach Stallings was standing in the middle of the exit ramp glaring at every player that went by.

At the top of the ramp stood a young manager, Lester Cox, directing us to a room. We all filed in and waited for Coach. None of us will ever forget what he did when he entered that room. He looked at one of the players—then grabbed him— and moved in, nose-to-nose. In this position, he gave him a short, intense little talk and then let go. He turned glaring at us. We braced for the worst. I remember exactly what he said because young impressionable minds don't forget times like that. "Men, you embarrassed Texas A&M tonight. You embarrassed your classmates, you embarrassed your mommas, you embarrassed your daddies, and you embarrassed your coaches. We will have no more of that in the future." Then Coach Stallings simply turned and left the room.

That big loss to TCU, and facing two of the best running backs (Bulaich and Montgomery) in Texas, made for a good initiation into college ball. The whole level of play was taken up a notch. Maybe three notches. This was more serious than what we had known as football.

Everyone had higher expectations. We were, in essence, being paid to play with the scholarships we had received. It was now more a job than just a high school "Friday night lights" hometown event.

And with the military background of Texas A&M came a sense of duty. Although A&M is no longer known for its corps of cadets, they wisely kept it central to the atmosphere. I am very thankful I played for A&M back then. It was tough. But looking back, I'm glad it was.

When I was a student, General Earl Rudder was President of Texas A&M. On the D-Day invasion of Normandy, June 6, 1944, he led the 2nd Ranger Battalion up the 100-foot cliffs above Omaha Beach at Pointe Du Hoc. Under withering fire from the Germans, his men suffered over 50% casualties on the first day of the assault, with over 100 killed in the first three days. Rudder, a Lt. Colonel at the time, was wounded twice but remained in action. He was one of 14 men in his battalion who were awarded the Distinguished Service Cross, the nation's highest award for bravery in combat, second only to the Medal of Honor.

As General Rudder stood on a platform one day before practice, his words pierced hearts. "Men, you are representing one of the greatest schools in the nation. Remember your heritage each time you run out on the practice field or game field. And know this: your fellow classmates have your back." This was one of those WWII warrior generals who had seen the worst and overcame the odds—a true patriot. By the way, my future wife, Janice, played with General Rudder's daughter, Linda Rudder, when he was the mayor of Brady, Texas, Janice's hometown. He would be proud today if he knew that Janice, about the time we were dating, seriously considered working

73

for the CIA.

You need men like General Rudder challenging your courage and perseverance. Football is a tough game. His talks helped us find a strength we didn't know we had.

CAN MAXWELL ROLL?

Funny story from my sophomore year at A&M.

Coach Stallings did not like to see injured players just standing around at practice. That meant that if you had some sort of injury, you needed to be doing something—or "sump'n" as Coach would say. So, if you were hurt, you could walk, ride a stationary bike, sit and lift your legs or arms—you could do "sump'n." Coach came from Paris, Texas, and he had a Texas drawl—with country slang thrown in.

Fellow wide receiver, Bob Long (19 touchdowns in 3 years) and I showed up hurt at the same practice and devised a plan to try and avoid "do'n sump'n."

Coach Stallings had a big tower that overlooked several football fields. Bob and I snuck under that tower so Coach Stallings couldn't see us. There we were, giggling and having fun under Coach's tower doing "nut'n" instead of "sump'n."

But, we had a curious trainer, Billy Pickard, who walked over to the tower and asked us what we were doing under there. This was a bad interruption to our plan! We tried our best using body language and hand motions to shoo him away, but he just stood there—looking at us—and talking to us! Then, from high

74

above, we heard something that brought wrath down upon us.

Through a loud megaphone we heard that voice, "Billy, who ya talkin' to?"

Billy responded, "Long and Maxwell, Coach."

"What're they doin' down there?"

"Well, Coach, Long has a bad shoulder and Maxwell has a pulled muscle."

Agonizing silence.

Then came the "creative healing gift" that few realize Coach Stallings has. He leaned over and boomed out, in his megaphone voice, "Can Maxwell roll?"

Billy said, "What'd you say, Coach?"

"I said, can...Maxwell...roll?"

"Yea, Coach, he can roll."

"Can Long walk? Or jog?"

"Yea, Coach, he can do both."

"Well, take Maxwell over to the other field and start him rolling, and I want Long running around him while he rolls."

Do you have that picture in your mind? Imagine it!

As Billy took us over to the other field, we pleaded with him in disbelief, "Billy, is Coach serious about this?" Billy just mumbled, "Yep. Now start rolling." We just couldn't believe it.

I got down, stretched out, arms by my side, legs extended— ready to roll. Bob denies this, but I remember him saying, "Tommy, let's get out of here and go play somewhere else. This is insanity." But we did it. Insane as it was.

After several rolls, all the way up and all the way back the length of the football field, I became very nauseated. Billy the

75

trainer came back after about twenty minutes and asked, "How you boys doing?" I said, "Billy, I can't do this for two hours!" And again, with all the compassion he could muster up, Billy said, "Well, Maxwell...roll slower." Soooo encouraging.

I always remind Coach Stallings about rolling when I get a chance to visit with him. I say, "Hey Coach, I saw another doctor last week and asked him if he has ever prescribed rolling as a 'cure all.'" Coach Stallings always gets a smile on his face. He knows what's coming. Then I say, "The doctor looked at me funny until I told him about how your 'rolling method' cured me overnight. I told him that I was at practice the next day!" Most doctors get a kick out of that true story...and so does Coach Stallings.

Those kinds of stories are funnier when you tell them than when you live them.

A BAD START

The first game of my junior year, we played Southern Methodist University at A&M. We should have won that game, our home opener, and we were picked by some sports writers to win the conference that year. It was a nationally televised game, I believe the first one of the year. Since then, I've talked to military Aggies (A&M was about one-third corps back than) who were in Vietnam and listened to that game on radio. I pictured some in fox holes, or at their posts, listening to the game! Aggies love their football.

In this game, my roommate, punter Steve O'Neal, faked a punt and threw me a pass which kept our drive going with just minutes left in the game. We eventually scored to take the lead, 17–13.

We kicked off. It was late in the fourth quarter. SMU had a wide receiver named Jerry LeVias (the first African American athlete to receive a scholarship at SMU or the SWC and later an NFL All-Pro) who not only handled the kickoff but gave SMU great field position on their own 42 yard line. The starting quarterback, Mike Livingston, was injured, so SMU had a backup quarterback named Ines Perez who took over. He was so short that his numbers were tucked into the back of his pants.

We thought this game was ours! Looks can be deceiving, though, and Mr. Perez proved that. He came into the game and completed 10 of 12 passes, including the game winner to Jerry Levias with 4 seconds left in the game. The papers called Perez a 5'4" "ball of fire!" He took SMU on a 58-yard touchdown drive for the score that beat us. It was really disappointing, but God had his purposes—always—even working in this game. SMU QB Ines Perez will come back later in my story as part of God's plan. No coincidences with God.

We went on to lose our first four games that year.

After the fourth loss, Coach Stallings announced to the team that, after repeated warnings, he kicked two of our starters off the team for not going to class. The team was shocked, but I believe the players respected Coach Stallings for that and, in a way, we all needed his wake-up call.

After the last loss, Coach Stallings called me into his office.

I wondered what he would say. Maybe that we would start passing more! After all, we had the best QB in the Conference, Ed Hargett, and a slew of good receivers, Barney Harris, Bob Long, Larry Lee, and Jimmy Adams. As it turned out—and this happened a lot—I didn't hear what I wanted to hear from Coach Stallings.

"Tommy, we are getting beat too much," he said, "and we want you to be like a free safety on defense and stay deep to stop the long passes. Can you help us there?"

What could I say? I still remembered his words when he recruited me, "You will come and help us, won't you?" Uh oh, Not So Fast showed up again—before I even got the nickname years later. On the spot, I agreed.

That day at practice, I became full-time on defense. Coach Stallings said that I would still have playing time at wide receiver. So maybe, I thought, this could be fun. I really kind of liked the challenge—at first. I left Coach Stallings' office thinking that I needed to try and intercept a few passes! That would be like a receiver on defense! Coach put a couple of other "good" offensive players on defense. One of them, Ross Brupbacher, went on to play for the Chicago Bears and became All-WFL (World Football League) in 1974.

We went on to win seven straight games and played against seventh-ranked Alabama in the Cotton Bowl. We were not even ranked at the time of the Cotton Bowl and picked to lose by 20 points! We beat Alabama 20 to 16. *Bebes and the Bear* is a good book about that "never give up" season, covering the Cotton

Bowl victory, with Gene "Bebes" Stallings' upstart Aggies gaining the victory over Bear Bryant's famed Crimson Tide.

Another important dynamic happened one rainy night after that fourth loss and after my visit with Coach Stallings. Someone we didn't recognize ran down the hallways of our dorm, Henderson Hall, hollering, "Come out to the front porch! Now!" One by one we poked our heads out of our rooms. Then a couple of players were shouting, "Get out here!" The rooms started emptying and when we went outside—I'll never forget what I saw.

There must have been a thousand (only ten thousand enrolled) students standing in the drizzly rain and our Yell Leaders (not called "Cheer Leaders" at A&M) were on the porch shaking our hands. Think about it: they did this after we lost our first four games. Which came after being picked to win the conference! Then, the Yell Leaders started with the organized yells unique to A&M. The whole team witnessed this unbelievable support. Big time losers...being treated like winners. President Rudder was right. Our students did have our back!

Again, more handshakes from the Yell Leaders and we went into the football dorm lounging area and had a team meeting. Several senior players shared their hearts that night. In essence, they all pointed to the incredible student support we witnessed. If these students were willing to stand in the rain at 9 p.m. and cheer for us after four losses, then we needed to do whatever it took to win the rest of our games. And we did. We won the next seven straight games to become the SWC Champions.

Those students that night showed commitment to us. They deeply inspired us. We were not even ranked after seven straight wins—and picked to lose the Cotton Bowl by 20 points! We went on to stomp Alabama pretty good. The takeaway from all of this: find a group of men who will commit to each other—and to a mission—and you will always find great accomplishments. Sounds like a Coaches Outreach Bible study group, doesn't it?

CHAPTER 6

TWIRLY BIRD
& PROF SMITH

SERIOUSLY BORED

Like high school, college filled my days with football and classes. I really wasn't thinking about dating. I did enjoy most of my classes and had fun with friends, but those friends didn't include girls really, because back in my day A&M was an all-male college. That was fine. I remembered the girl in high school who wanted to take up a lot of my time. That wasn't a problem here, although I did have a friend on the team who was dating a girl at Baylor University. I remember thinking that all the Baylor girls seemed pretty. And, I should mention, Baylor was about an hour drive from A&M.

One Sunday evening, in my junior year (1967), about 6:30 p.m., my friend was talking to his girlfriend on the phone. As I walked into his room, he handed the phone to me. That hadn't happened before. *Hmmm. What's up?* I wondered. His girlfriend asked me if I could bring my friend to Baylor, since his car was in the shop. Long drive, I thought.

But then again, for a guy who thrived on excitement, I was seriously bored. There was nothing to do in Bryan-College Station back then, and so I thought I would just go and walk around the Baylor campus. It would be better than just sitting around our dorm.

I told her, "OK, we're comin'." And then she said, "And Tommy, I'm going to get you a date."

OK, hold it right there. Not interested in a date. And I told her that in no uncertain terms. "Look. I don't want a date. No way." I already had a plan, I told her—very clearly. "I'll drive, then I'll give you two the car, and I'll go find something to do by myself. That's the plan."

But then, when we picked up my friend's date, she told me she set up a date for me. What? I was not happy about it and said I wouldn't go. She replied, "Well, I've already set it up and she's waiting to meet you." Great. It was almost like getting orders from Coach Stallings' tower. What could I do? I reluctantly agreed to go on the date. A blind date, as they say.

We went to another girl's dormitory to meet "my date." And a girl showed up at the top of the stairs.

BAYLOR BEAUTY

A really pretty girl with big brown eyes. She came down the stairs, smiling and looking toward us. I sure hoped she was "my date." I got my wish. And right away we had something in common.

This girl didn't want to go on a date either! She actually never accepted the date—her roommate accepted for her. She needed to study, it was late, and she didn't have time for a date. Her roommate persisted, adding, "He plays football for A&M." My date remarked, "I don't date football players." However, she did agree to go—reluctantly.

Of course, I didn't know she wasn't happy about the date. She came over and introduced herself. Janice Breckenridge. And I was thinking, "Not bad for a last minute blind date!" I drove my friend and his date to a park in Waco. Janice and I got out of the car and we walked around visiting.

There was something about her. This girl was different.

That date kept coming back to my mind during those seven straight wins (after four straight losses) that season. But, the focus was now football since we had started winning. Yet, as involved as I was, I kept thinking about Janice Breckenridge.

She was a beautiful girl. A beautiful person, too. I would later learn that Janice was a twirler at Brady High School. And at Baylor, she was a Golden Girl twirler for the band (gold and green were the Baylor colors). Once again, God's sovereign plan was at work, his providence in action, moving behind the scenes.

We had gone out a couple of times. Later in the football season, Janice invited me to a beauty contest. This was the final portion of a pageant where each of the "beauties" strolled across the stage. I don't remember her saying she was in the contest—but she was—and I'll never forget when Janice stepped out on that stage. An older lady next to me actually gasped, "Oh my, that girl is the prettiest girl here!" I kept my tongue, but I wanted to turn to her and say, "Guess who the prettiest girl is going out with tonight?"

Not until after we married did I find out: Janice loves football! Back in college, when she heard more about me, and discovered I was a wide receiver, she grew a little more curious. She did—and does—love the game of football. I mean, she's glued to it. That girl, my date, to this day, still loves watching the ball being thrown and caught. She still screams at exciting catches on TV! You'd better be ready for it. I remember bolting up from a nice nap one afternoon when Janice jumped to her feet and yelled at the television! I learned I'd better be ready for it.

Hey, what can I say? From the start, it was a providential matchup and we both know who divinely planned that date. A sovereign God brought us together—for now and eternity.

TWIRLY BIRD

Thankfully, we had two or three wins after the four straight losses—and very thankfully—we had a weekend off. A Saturday without a game.

I found out that Baylor had a home game. I wanted to see Janice again. This could be the perfect time. "Shoot," I said, "If I leave now, I can make it by halftime." Hey, some excitement!

I arrived just before halftime, bought a ticket, and searched out where the Baylor twirlers were sitting. The twirlers were about to perform, so I went to the Baylor band's area where they all sat, and where they'd come back after their performance.

I waited by myself. I did feel kinda funny. I mean, it was just me, there on those empty benches. Another fast decision from Not So Fast himself. I didn't think about it, watching the people in the band perform, and one particular twirler who really caught my eye: Janice.

Soon after the twirlers' performance, she showed up. She came toward me, baton in hand, and stopped. Uh, oh. She gave me a look. You know, a look that says, "What?" meaning, "Tommy? What are you doing here?"

Well, for over 52 years now, I've had a lot of those looks. I told her I came to see her twirl. I wish I could have been more cool about it. As the seconds ticked by, I felt more and more awkward. Some of her twirly-bird girlfriends were giggling and looking at me.

Now, if you are an Aggie (from the "all-male" A&M days) you're probably smiling, remembering your own different dating situations back in those days. Sometimes, you drove a long way to have a date with a young lady, since they didn't often show up on campus, and if they did, they were probably already taken. Today when I visit A&M, I see pretty girls all over the campus. That's a change! And by pretty girls, I include my granddaughter, Kate, who is not just pretty, she's gorgeous. (OK, a little granddad bias here).

85

I watched the game, sitting there with the band members and twirlers, and worked up the courage to ask Janice for dinner. Whew, she said, "Yes."

We went to a steak place where I gobbled down my steak. She had only eaten half of hers and then stopped. By reflex, I went back to my crude training table roots (grab for the last bite of anything), took my fork and reached out to her piece of steak, saying, "I guess you're through with this." The fork touched down and in an instant, she calmly took her fork and stuck it in the back of my hand! Enough for me to want to say "Ouch!" Then, in a nice sweet voice she said, "I'm not through." Needless to say, I pulled back. There was a moment of silence, and she cut a piece of steak, and ate it, very ladylike. *I like this girl*, I thought.

Soon after that, I met her parents and later had her sit with my parents at the Cotton Bowl—after losing our first four games and winning seven straight ones (just reminding you). That was the first time I had ever asked a date to come to a game. Something was different about this girl.

A SPECIAL BUNCH OF MEN

In 2010, I had the privilege of being one of the speakers at a "roast" for Coach Stallings in Alabama. After I told my rolling story, I shared how Coach Stallings helped turn our team around, which led to the story of us winning the Cotton Bowl. Then I sat down.

The next speaker, Coach Pat Dye (College Hall of Fame coach) came to the podium. He looked over at me and said, "Tommy, I remember well that 1968 Cotton Bowl game against Texas A&M. I can remember sitting in the Alabama locker room before that game (Coach Dye was an assistant coach at Alabama then) and looking at the game program along with another coach."

Coach Dye told the audience that when he saw the scarred-up faces of all the A&M boys, he said to the other coach, "These guys may just beat the snot out of us today."

I wished that our whole A&M team from back then could have been in the audience and heard a great man like Coach Dye say that. Our players were good—not great—but they would come after you for 60 minutes straight. What a special bunch of men. God would later give me the privilege to play for some great teams, but none as great as the Texas A&M 1968 Cotton Bowl champs.

Funny side story from that Cotton Bowl victory. Rick Rickman and Lester Cox were student managers for A&M back then. We players now call them our "lifetime managers" because they have always been there for us players…after all these years.

Here is what happened. After the game, Coach Stallings told Rick to guard the door. He pressed his point: "Do not allow anyone to come into the locker room!" Well, guess who showed up knocking at the door? Alabama's coach, Bear Bryant. Rick told him what Coach Stallings had said and Coach Bryant said, with authority, "I'm not just anyone! Open this door!" Guess who came in? And, maybe for the first time in history, a legendary coach (maybe any kind of coach) came into the locker room of the opposing team who had won—and shook hands with every player.

Writing this now, it still makes me teary-eyed, just thinking how cool that was. On top of that, we left the dressing room to be greeted by a clapping and grateful crowd. It seems like yesterday.

But there was one person in the crowd I was most excited to see. Yeah, you guessed it. Janice, my future wife. The blind date. The twirl girl. The fork girl. The first girl I had ever invited to any football game. I liked and dated a lot of different girls, but as I've told you, there was just something unusual I felt about this girl. That unusual feeling I now clearly recognize after 52 years of marriage. And it's still there. Love.

Janice was excited to see me too, but she was thrilled about the pass I caught in the game. Just the other day she was telling someone about it, like it was yesterday. "Tommy caught this incredible pass. He ran and jumped at least three feet in the air, hands reaching high, catching that ball in the end zone for a touchdown. He made an interception, too, but that one catch helped A&M win the Cotton  Bowl!" Scan this QR code for Tommy's sports videos and interviews.

ALL-AMERICAN PUNTER

My roommate at A&M was Steve O'Neal, our punter. Since I never had a brother, I adopted Steve as my brother. Steve had gone to A&M on a track scholarship as a hurdler. He had been the punter for his high school but had not been recruited for college football. Coach Watson heard from Steve's high school coach that Steve was a really good punter. Coach Watson watched Steve punt and recommended him to Coach Stallings. At first, Coach was skeptical about a track guy punting for the team. But that opinion changed when, one day, he saw Steve booming that ball so far down the field.

I used to stay after practice and catch Steve's punts on occasion. I've kiddingly reminded him that I helped him become an All-American punter. He would easily kick the ball 70 yards, time after time! He could have had the highest average in college yardage ever, but he had to punt the ball from the opponent's 40 yard line since we had no long field goal kickers. Steve learned how to punt the ball toward the sideline, landing the ball inside the 10 yard line where it would hit and go straight out. It was really amazing. He could keep the other team deep in their territory that way. I even stopped a few punts down inside the 5 for him since I was an outside man on the punt team. Steve was voted an All-American punter our senior year.

Later, Steve played professional football for the New York Jets and the New Orleans Saints. He still has the National Football League record for the longest punt: 98 yards. That record will never be broken because the NFL only measures punts

89

from the 1 to the 1 yard line. The other amazing thing about Steve is that he went to dental school in the offseason while he played pro football. He is now retired as the best dentist ever in Bryan-College Station, Texas. I'm a little biased. Just a little.

RUNNING FULL SPEED

Lloyd Taylor was an assistant coach at Texas A&M during my playing years. He was also a Junction Boy, one of the players at Bear Bryant's tough 10-day summer camp in Junction, Texas. He was small in stature but big in presence. In my senior year at Texas A&M, Coach Taylor called me up to him just after we had finished a few 100-yard sprints after practice. He said, "Tommy, I want you to stay out here when the team goes in." That sounded serious.

Well, after everyone was gone he said, "I want you to run some more hundreds." What? I just finished running hundreds. Back then, you didn't question authority, so I didn't ask why. However, I never had a coach say that before. Coach Taylor then said, "I want you to get down and, on my whistle, I want you to run 100 yards full speed to the end of the field. When you get to the end, I want you to get down, with no rest and, on my whistle, come back to me full speed—100%. You understand?" "Yes sir."

Well, being the good faker I was, I decided to just look like I was going 100%. So, I took off with a strained look at about 70% because there was no way I was going to run full speed,

90

not knowing how many hundreds of this drill I would have to run.

When I got back, Coach Taylor said, "Tommy, did you not understand me? I said to go full speed and you are just cruising. Now, get down!" Gosh, I can't remember a coach ever getting on me like that. So, this time I gutted it out at 80% since I was breathing hard and again thinking I better hold back a little since he hadn't let me rest at all. Surely, the coach would say after I came back this time, "That's more like it, Tommy." Then, I guessed, he would give me a little talk about effort, and send me in. Did not happen. When I got back after my fourth 100-yard sprint, he was glaring at me.

"Tommy, I have all day and all night, so just keep screwing around and we'll see the sun go down and the moon come up. Do you like to run in the dark?" Uh, oh...he's serious...and mad. I never saw Coach Taylor like that—not at me anyway. "Get down," he said.

Off I went on his whistle, and now I was really breathing hard. There was no way could I go 100%. Again, no rest after the fifth 100-yard dash and then that dang whistle to come back. Now, when I came back, I was gasping for air. Then I heard it again, "Get down!" *Good night*, I thought. *I might die out here!*

Now—I was ticked. He got to me. I had thoughts of punching my coach, but I was way too tired for that. This time, in anger, I gave it all I had up and back—for the first time in my life. When I got back after the eighth 100-yard dash, I had a hard time standing up.

91

"Listen," Coach Taylor said, "I've been watching you. You slide in with the lineman when we do our 100-yard runs after practice." *Oooh, he's got me.* "You have a chance to play some pro ball, but you will never make it if you are just trying to get by on minimum effort." Then I heard something that really sunk in. Coach Taylor said, "Tommy, why didn't you run that hard at the beginning? If you had run just two 100s at full speed, that would have been enough."

That day, Coach Taylor gave me a new life in the physical sense. He showed me that I could do a lot more than I ever thought I could. He had to get me mad to do it, but I'm thankful. It was a turning point. And once again, I credit my sovereign God bringing that event into my life. Was it coincidence that Coach Taylor was moved to challenge me that day, in that way? No, it was not coincidence. There are no coincidences.

God is sovereign and in control of all, even Coach Taylor's challenge. Throughout the Bible, God has used all kinds of people, even people not committed to him—think of Pharaoh, Pilate, or those who crucified Jesus. He has used those kinds of people to accomplish his will and his ways. I was not yet a believer in a personal Savior, but I learned so much from that experience. As you can see, I've never forgotten it!

The harder the lesson, the longer it stays with you.

BETTER AT SPORTS—BETTER AT LIFE

You know, I've discovered over the years that every player

who went through a coach's "grinder" has not only become better at sports, but better at life. Coaching is about people doing their best physically, not just about winning. No one team or one player wins all the time, right?

In fact, most fans in our society are so insecure, they demand winning from their team so they can feel that they are winners too! If their team loses, they feel like losers. They identify completely with a team. From a biblical perspective, this is really a form of idolatry—finding your worth in something or someone (a team, your work, your house, your car, your children, etc.) rather than God. Yet, most people have never been in the arena, giving their all with their teammates, inspired by their efforts.

Playing sports is about working hard and wanting to win. I mean, enjoying the challenge, not just winning. Becoming better at a sport, encouraging one another, setting realistic goals, protecting one another, and learning what your 100% is all about—that is what makes any sporting event exciting and fulfilling.

Anyone can buy players or recruit players that are naturally better athletes. You get enough of them and you will win. But winning is not what being in sports is all about. Here's something else about players who go through a coach's "grinder." They go on to be successful in whatever they do—whether they ever played a down of football while at A&M or not. They are all winners in my eyes. Become better at sports; become better at life.

JUNCTION BOYS

Most of our coaches at A&M, including Coach Stallings, were part of the Junction Boys camp I mentioned, under Coach Bear Bryant. You need to read the best-selling book *The Junction Boys* by Jim Dent (also a movie) to fully understand their mindset. And, as I mentioned, Coach Stallings and his coaches were all just about 29 years old when they started coaching us at A&M.

Most people don't realize the pressure that comes with coaching at a major college like Texas A&M. It's really the same at the high school level. That kind of pressure, when you're a young coach and not used to it, can make you inflexible, uptight, insensitive, and blindly focused—all symptoms of the relentless pressure to win. It's quite common for coaches to put in 16-hour days. It takes a toll on the body. Young college players (our nonstarters mostly) were at times ignored by tired coaches, who were just trying to survive. But, even the players who quit the team and chose "college only," will admit that they found they could do a lot more than they thought they could.

All my former teammates have become successful even if they left A&M with bitter feelings. I have been able to talk with just about all the coaches from our team back then and I believe their deepest desire was for each of us see that we could do a lot more than we thought we could—on and off the field.

But, they would admit, there was very little encouragement with the testing we were all put through. To turn a very weak football program around takes some painful confrontation—

even though it would deeply hurt some—and wasn't fair to others. To turn a losing team around and win the Southwest Conference (SWC) in three years, then beat Alabama in the Cotton Bowl, took young men who had been tested. That's why, to me, Army boot camp looked like nothing compared to our A&M football training!

Bear Bryant's philosophy came through. That was, "You must have players who are going as strong in the fourth quarter as they are in the first." I have a deep respect for all the young men who were part of the team back then, even if they were only on the team a month or two. Once a teammate, always a teammate, and we all helped each other become better, one way or another.

We had a sign over the exit door to the practice field that we each saw every day:

MAKE SOMETHING HAPPEN

That fit my personality. I had to learn, however, that making something happen without understanding God's sovereignty is not really that exciting. Put that saying along with scripture reading, praying, and submitting to God's will on a daily basis, and you will see the power of a sovereign God to give you a powerful and purposeful life.

I know some of the guys who, rightly so, still resent the disrespectful way they felt they were treated. However, holding resentment only hurts one person. I had my share of being pushed, but it was good for me. I needed to toughen up and be challenged. And God put Gene Stallings and his coaching staff in my life to do just that. It may sound corny, but I really do—even all these years later—love and respect all my coaches.

But there was one man in my life who was, I guess you could say, an "eternal coach," who prepared me for more than just life. He prepared me for the life to come.

PROF SMITH: GAME CHANGER

Probably the biggest part of my junior year, well, the biggest part of my time at A&M—and the most significant change of my entire life—was meeting a man nicknamed "Prof Smith." Another perfectly timed man (coach) that God brought into my life.

Prof Smith was a professor before he became the pastor of a small country church. A big difference in his ministry came from the fact that he didn't really preach sermons based on the Bible; he taught what was in the Bible, sometimes called expository teaching or verse-by-verse teaching. It was different—and deeper.

God brought to these football players an older, energetic, but nonathletic Bible coach who made Scripture come alive in our hearts. And it was easy to know why he could. Because Jesus was alive in Prof's heart. It was like Jesus shined right through him, showing God's love to these rugged athletes. And instead of Prof expecting us players to come to him, he came to us—where we lived—in the dorm. Yes, I said *us*. Although, at first, I just watched from the outside.

I would see players listening to Prof as he taught them the Bible, but I didn't feel comfortable joining them. I didn't know anything about the Bible. We all liked Prof Smith because he would meet and greet different players like myself and make good conversation. He had a great spirit about him. I guess you could say, I was drawn to him. Especially one specific night.

I was reading a book of philosophy during that football comeback year on a Sunday night, and—I know this—God's Spirit spoke to me to go see Prof Smith. It wasn't an audible voice, but a strong sense. An impulse I couldn't resist.

I know now—though I didn't know then—that God can do what he wants, when he wants, to whomever he chooses. It was like I was levitated from my bed to go and talk to Prof. I didn't know his number, so I just went to his house about 9 p.m. I knocked on his door.

A minute passed and then the door opened. He greeted me. "Hey Tommy, how are you doing?"

I answered, "Hey Prof, I hate to be here at this hour, but I don't know anything about the Bible and I want to learn. Can you teach me, one-on-one, sometime?"

Prof Smith perked up and I was surprised when he said, "Sure, let's start tonight. Do you like history?"

I said I did and he said, "Come on in and I'll give you a quick Bible history lesson."

God made me to like history. It has always fascinated me. Prof didn't know that. God did, of course. I mean, this whole experience was supernatural. Or, more accurately, God-or-dained. It was clear: God was working through Prof to grab my attention. I couldn't explain why I wanted to learn the Bible, but I always had a sense of a big God up there, looking out for me.

God was up there, in his world; I was "down here" in mine. I did not have what I'd later call a personal relationship with God. I rarely thought about spiritual things because I was occupied with football and just focused on other stuff. I did say the Lord's Prayer every night, more as a good luck charm than with any meaning. But God had a plan. He stopped me in my tracks—before I got any further. You got it, another Not So Fast moment!

So, there in his home, for the next 30 minutes, Prof started with Genesis, reading "In the beginning..." and going on to show me the history of Jesus throughout the Old Testament.

He then went to the New Testament, where John the Baptist said, "Behold the lamb of God, who takes away the sins of the world!" (John 1:29).

He asked me, "Who do you think John is pointing out?"

Since we were in the New Testament and Prof had shown me the coming Savior in the Old Testament, I answered, "Jesus Christ."

"Right answer, Tommy," he replied.

That made me feel good. It was the perfect lead-in to his invitation. He asked if I wanted to receive Christ as my Lord and Savior. I did. Prof Smith led me in a prayer and from that moment on, my life would be changed forever.

When I got back in my car, I just sat there for five minutes. There were no bells or whistles. All was quiet as I reflected on what had just happened. I had a sense that I had done something very important.

I didn't realize that the Holy Spirit had come to be my Helper. "But the Helper, the Holy Spirit whom the Father will send in My name, He will teach you all things, and remind you of all things that I said to you" (John 14:26 NKJV).

The Holy Spirit is the Helper who generates life and purpose, maintaining our connection with the Father and the Son. This Scripture is an honest, trustworthy promise from God, and through this understanding, I know that his Son and his Scripture have given me new life, new purpose, and a greater understanding of our Creator. Since those five reflective moments— to this very day—I live with a fresh desire to know and understand God's truth.

In that short "history lesson" with Prof Smith, my life was intercepted by the reality and presence of God. My new life with God is the same, all these years later, each and every day. This verse rings true: "Jesus Christ is the same yesterday and today and forever" (Hebrews 13:8).

Everything had changed. My thinking, my worldview, my goals—everything. Not all at once, I suppose, but over time, the Holy Spirit was working in me to make me more like Christ.

Recently, on a Sunday morning, our pastor mentioned the Westminster Shorter Catechism. It sums up the purpose and goal of my life, and of every believer, and what we should always be going for. It's "The Big Play," you could say, with an even bigger touchdown: "The chief end of man is to glorify God and to enjoy him forever."

I was blessed by the Lord with many highlights in my sports career and several honors across the years. Since you asked—well, I guess you didn't—here are some highlights from my career before going pro:

All-Southwest Conference (now SEC) Freshman Wide Receiver, 1965.

All-Southwest Conference Varsity WR, 1966–68.

All-American Defensive Back, 1968.

Post--season College All-Star game in Chicago, Illinois and the Senior Bowl game in Mobile, Alabama, both in 1969.

Texas A&M Hall of Fame, 1991.

CHAPTER 7
BALTIMORE COLT #42

COLLEGE ALL-STAR GAME

After my senior college football season ended, I was invited to play in the Senior Bowl. When I played, back in 1969, the Senior Bowl was also called "the North/South game." I played on the South team and we lost the game that year. Two other players from Texas A&M, Rolf Krueger and Edd Hargett, were also invited to play.

I also played in the College All-Star game in Chicago. Some of the players tried to set me up to date some girls from Chicago, but I just wasn't interested. And I hadn't seen Janice due to these two games, so I got this idea.

Shoot, I thought, *I'm getting about a thousand dollars for playing in this game* (this brought me into pro status). *I can pay for Janice's travel expenses and fly her to Chicago.*

So, I called Janice and I invited her to the game, which was the second time for an invited girlfriend in my game history.

She accepted! When I met her at the airport, it hit the ol' slow poke—me—and I thought, *I've really missed this girl.*

After she checked into the same hotel where the team was staying, I went to her room to pick her up and take her out to dinner.

A METHODIST AND A BAPTIST

I can still see what happened next. The big moment. But at the wrong time. While Janice fixed her hair, and I sat on the bed, words began coming out of my mouth—and there was no way to take them back.

"Say," I started, "I'm a Methodist and you're a Baptist. How will that work when we're married?"

There was a moment of silence and, once again, like the time she saw me sitting there in the bleachers at the Baylor game, I saw that "What?" expression on her face.

"Is that a proposal?" She asked.

My cool answer: "I suppose it is." My face probably looked like a confused question mark.

The conversation dropped pretty quickly. It was awkward, and for her, of course, completely unexpected. I don't think I'd ever said, "I love you" or anything like that. Although one time we were together with one of my buddies and, without really thinking about it, I casually said, "Ya know, this person right here, Janice, this is the girl I'm going to ask to marry me." Probably got the face then, too. Awkward.

Janice and I did have a nice dinner that evening. No wedding talk, though in my mind it was a sealed deal. I remember

102

calling my parents later and telling them about the proposal, and the Methodist-Baptist approach. "That's nice," is about all I got from them.

The day after the game, when I took Janice to the airport, she looked at me and said, "So. Are we engaged?"

I said, "Sure! I guess I need to get you an engagement ring. Should I go get it, or do you want us to get it together?"

"Let's get it together," she replied.

Looking back, as I write this, I realize how much I "blew it," messing up such a special moment. But we were both happy, and the wedding plans had begun. Romantic, huh?

A BALTIMORE COLT

Backing up the story to the spring of my senior year at A&M, I received a call from the Dallas Cowboys football office. They wanted me and my roommate, Steve O'Neal, to come to the Dallas Cowboys office for testing.

The Dallas Cowboys! My dream team! Steve and I were pumped! I believed the Dallas Cowboys were going to draft me in the first round of the pro football draft. Naive, I know, but I'm all about excitement. Let's face it: excitement is kind of like the wind. It can blow out as quickly as it blows in.

I wasn't picked in the first round of the NFL draft by Dallas—or any other team. I sure thought the Cowboys would've wanted me…what a disappointment for a naive 21 year old.

Janice happened to visit me in Houston. After the first-round picks, I told Janice, "Let's go to the mall." Well, that was kind of a knee-jerk reaction, but I had to get away. Had to walk around. Had to process what just happened to me.

I told Janice, I just figured that since the Cowboys had invited Steve and me to meet with them, we would both go in the first round. It seemed like a done deal. She listened as we walked past the stores. And, out of nowhere—my dad showed up. I couldn't remember my dad ever going to the mall. "What are you doing here?" I asked, probably with a confused look on my face.

Dad said it plain and simple, "Tommy, you are now a Baltimore Colt."

"What?!" I shot back.

"You went in the second round," he said.

All I knew about the Colts was that Johnny Unitas was their quarterback and Raymond Berry was Johnny's favorite receiver. In fact, as a kid, I spent hours in my yard being Johnny U and Raymond Berry. I would be Johnny Unitas, coming under the center and calling out an audible. Then I would drop back as Johnny U, and being my own commentator, say, "Unitas drops back—he sees Berry open—he launches the ball!" And I would throw the football high enough and long enough for Raymond (me) to run under and catch it. I would then say something like, "Berry makes another great catch!" Kept myself entertained for hours that way! Now, I was Johnny Unitas' teammate. For real.

And on the first day of regular season football (preseason was over and squad chosen), I was walking to our first practice and Johnny U came up beside me, put his arm around me, and said, "Tommy, I'm glad you're a Colt." I can still feel that Golden Arm around my shoulders. Johnny actually owned a popular restaurant in Baltimore called the Golden Arm. It was indeed the golden moment of all my football days.

Another great moment, many years later, was when, as founder of Coaches Outreach, I called Raymond Berry. I introduced myself, mentioned our connection as former Baltimore Colts, and explained our ministry and how we wanted to reach out to junior and senior high coaches. Raymond was a strong Christian. In fact, he and Don Shinnick started the pregame chapel service for the Colts that most teams have today. I asked him if he would speak at our first Coaches Outreach banquet. He said he'd do it! I was so excited. I drove to the airport and watched for him as people came off the plane. I just couldn't believe it when I saw him walk into the waiting area. Right there. Johnny Unitas' favorite receiver! And I was him, hehe, when I was my own commentator! Even as I write this, I just shake my head when I think of God's sovereign goodness to make my childhood dream come alive.

Walking out of the airport with Raymond Berry was like walking with Chuck Swindoll (definitely another hero of mine) to the airport, in my days at Dallas Theological Seminary, and walking on that practice field with Johnny Unitas. Johnny and me: a hero and a rookie.

One more story about Raymond at the Coaches Outreach banquet. On my way to the hotel banquet room, I saw Raymond in the restaurant. I went over to him and noticed he had

105

3x5 note cards arranged across the table. Looking closer, I realized they were Bible verses. He explained that these were his memory verses. Memory verses?

Yep, another life-impacting moment. Raymond shared his goals for scripture memory, and remembering that makes me want to get together with Harv Cox, a close friend here in Granbury. Harv would never boast about it, but when I questioned him, he said he could bring up 300 verses when he needed to. And he loves to help other Christians memorize God's Word. And you know what I've concluded? Memorizing scripture keeps you young. Harv is 87 and looks 67!

Back to the Baltimore Colts. As it turned out, they drafted me as a defensive back. Hmm. I never really liked that position, but I hung around for six years in pro ball, since I could also play wide receiver and catch punts. All my pro coaches had me learn offensive plays—just in case. I only played at wide receiver a few times during preseason games. I caught a few passes, but never played during the regular season. To this day, I really consider myself an offensive player. Anyway, for being Not So Fast, I'm actually getting ahead of myself.

ROOKIE YEAR

It was July 1969, the summer camp of my rookie year with the Baltimore Colts.

The Colts held their preseason camp in California, at Cal Poly College in San Luis Obispo, midway between San Jose and

Los Angeles. We practiced in Mustang Stadium, and the first day of practice was brutal. The recorded temperature for that day was 104 degrees, and we practiced without pads. Misery on top of misery.

After practice, I heard Coach Bobby Boyd, my coach at the Colts, say it was time to run gassers after practice. I turned to one of the veterans and asked, "What's a gasser?"

"Well," he explained, "one gasser is four 50s going across the football field and back twice."

I took off like a gazelle and finished my last 50 yards about 50 yards ahead of the other players. One of the veterans came over to scold me, "Tommy, we don't run them that fast. Slow down."

Like all the rookies, we were kind of afraid of the veterans and overachieved to make a good impression.

Coach Boyd also said to slow down. But I remembered A&M's Coach Taylor and those last two 100-yard sprints I ran the previous fall. I could still hear Coach Taylor counseling me, "Tommy, you have a chance to play some pro ball, but you will never make it if you are just trying to get by on minimum effort."

I took off on the next gasser as if Coach Taylor was still glaring at me. The veterans were now trying to stay up. God used Coach Taylor—again—to make me take a good look at a real weakness—just getting by on God-given skills. I learned that I had to give my full effort to whatever I was doing.

Coach Boyd was a great coach. An All-Pro defensive back with the Baltimore Colts, he became an All-Pro because he played smart. As a former college quarterback at Oklahoma, he studied the game. He was a ferocious tackler, strange for a former quarterback. The Colts played mostly zone defense back then (focus on an area, not just one receiver), so Coach Boyd's smarts in reading pass patterns and getting a jump on the ball became the key to his success with the old Baltimore Colts.

Coach Boyd taught me the game. I was a typical rookie player. I made a lot of mistakes, but he never harped on that. Instead, he encouraged me. I needed that because, as I said, I never really liked being a defensive back. It seemed that I became more and more tight, or pressured, after becoming a starter in the seventh game of my rookie season. I did put way too much pressure on myself. I just didn't have the temperament for that position. For me, it was actually much harder than playing wide receiver.

I couldn't stand it when a receiver caught a ball on me. It drove me nuts each time. However, as with any NFL defensive back, receivers are going to catch balls on you. The receivers do have an advantage. I knew that intellectually, but I wanted it to be me making the big catch. I just couldn't accept receivers catching balls on me. I was a hard hitter, but not a very good open field tackler. That's a skill all to itself.

Scan this QR code for Tommy's sports videos and interviews.

SLICK SPOTS

Since Lenny Lyles was playing his last year with the Colts, they groomed me to take his place at right cornerback. Lenny was a class guy, and when they started me in his place, the seventh game of my rookie year (started next seven games), Lenny was always there to help me. I would come off the field and he'd come over and coach me on just about everything I confronted. I'll always love Lenny for that.

I hated the pressure of lining up across All-Pro receivers. In my first professional football game, I was covering All-Pro and Hall of Fame player, Charley Taylor of the Washington Redskins. I guess I was not that nervous since I didn't know what to expect. I do remember him running a down-and-out pattern and thinking, "I'm all over this!"

And, sure enough, I was! I intercepted it! I thought to myself, *Hey, this ain't so hard.*

Little did I know that I would be facing four more All-Pros that season. Somewhere in there came Carroll Dale with the Green Bay Packers and Bob Hayes with the Dallas Cowboys. "Bullet Bob" Hayes, also an Olympic gold medalist sprinter, caught a long pass on me. I was glad when that moment was over. But it came up again, years later, talking to a neighbor (also a big football fan) who asked me about it—and then recounted it to me in vivid detail. Ouch.

Yeah, cocky, first game Interception Boy had some things to learn. It was like those vets watched that Redskin game against Charley Taylor and said to themselves, "I got this

109

rookie. He won't be intercepting me!"

Yep, the very next game I was covering Carroll Dale of the Green Bay Packers. I had him man-for-man on one play with no help. He came down straight at me and then swerved to my inside a little. Then, with a head fake to the outside, I went down, and Carroll Dale took off. What a panicky and sick feeling. I jumped up and started chasing him. He had to slow down to catch the ball, and I was able to catch up and bring him down. It was about a 40-yard gain, but I don't remember if the Packers went on to score or not.

I came to the sideline and one of the coaches handed me his headphones, saying, "Coach Boyd wants to talk to you from the press box."

I put on the headphones and heard Coach Boyd say, "I want you to look out there on our 40 yard line about 15 yards in and tell me what you see."

I was straining to see but couldn't see a thing. "Coach, I don't see anything."

"Keep looking," he said.

"Coach, there looks like a little dark spot out there, but that's all I see."

"Tommy, that little dark spot is a muddy slick spot, and Carroll Dale ran you right into it. He made a head fake so you would plant your foot to cut, and that's when your foot slipped and you went down. You're in the pros now, Tommy, and the smart receivers will know where all the slick places are. You better know where they are, too."

Christians need to know where Satan's slick places are. We

don't have 100,000 people watching us slip and fall, but our Lord is watching—and we live in front of a watching world. We need to "walk the field," studying God's truth and staying on our feet, firmly planted on God's wisdom. Our enemy's slick spots, "the schemes of the devil" (Ephesians 6:11), include robbing our lives of the fruit of the spirit (Galatians 5:22-23) and replacing those qualities with human feelings as we live life for self instead of for God and others. Let's study the Scripture, God's "playbook and films." Through consistent study and reflection, Jesus will make us winners with fruitful and purposeful lives.

Like Coach Boyd, the apostle Peter warned us, "Be soberminded; be watchful. Your enemy the devil prowls around like a roaring lion, seeking someone to devour" (1 Peter 5:8).

Carroll Dale devoured me! The modern football fan has a hard time picturing this with all the indoor stadiums and artificial turf. There are no slick spots anymore. Back in my day, they would cover the grass fields with pulled-together tarps. If you had a good deal of rain, some of the rainwater would run off in places where two tarps didn't join together, and a slick spot was born!

Yep, I learned a lot under Coach Bobby Boyd. He was smarter than most receivers he covered and that is how, as a non-speedy defensive back, he became All-Pro.

Thanks to Coach Boyd, I started walking the field before every game to check for anything that could trip me up.

FACE TO FACE WITH PARDEE

I can remember a couple of rookie incidences that same year. Two vivid memories happened in two games.

I was face to face with Coach Jack Pardee in a game against the LA Rams in the old Memorial Los Angeles Coliseum (now SoFi Stadium). Coach Pardee was a former Junction Boy with Coach Stallings at A&M, a future college and NFL coach, and an All-Pro linebacker with the Rams my rookie year. Coach Stallings had Jack Pardee come and help coach the defense during spring training my junior year at A&M. One day, Pardee tried to get a point across to one of our defensive lineman who kept making the same mistake. Coach Pardee put his hands under the armpits of the lineman and literally picked him up off the ground—calmly talking to him as he held him in the air! That's all our team could talk about for days.

Now, fast forward about 15 months. I was a rookie with the Baltimore Colts and positioned as one of the end men facing outward on a field goal attempt. As I lined up for a field goal, guess who stood over me swinging his arm and glaring at me. Yep, Coach "Holding Up That Lineman" Pardee. He calmly said to me while swinging his right arm (yes, I remember and see that arm even today), "Tommy—I am going to take your head right off your body." All I remember is pulling my shoulder pads up as high as I could and putting myself in the tightest position humanly possible. The ball snapped and the kick was over. And there I was, still looking like a frozen humanoid. And do you know what happened next? Coach Pardee took one step toward me, patted me on the head, and said, "Relax man, I was just kidding." That was not funny at the time. I could hardly relax—even after he said that! I gave him a half-smile as he turned to walk away. I think I heard him giggle.

GET ME TO THE CHURCH ON TIME

The head coach of the Baltimore Colts, Don Shula ran a tight ship. I remember, early on with the Colts, when I went to my locker for the first time. Right there, at my locker, Tom Matte gave me the lowdown on Shula. Tom called me "Rook" (for rookie) from our first meeting. I loved Tom Matte, who went on to become a veteran player.

Turns out, there were some lines you didn't cross with this coach. Rule #1: Never miss team meetings. Rule #2: Be at practice on time. Without really meaning to, I was about to break both rules. Blame it on a little thing called marriage.

So in love with my college sweetheart, Janice, I decided to get married in the middle of the season. This was going to be rough with Coach Shula's rules about practice. But we decided to go forward with it. We set the wedding for right after our game with the New Orleans Saints (closest game to Janice's hometown of Brady, Texas).

We had already picked out the rings after the Houston Oiler game a couple of weeks before. I talked to a friendly cab driver at a hotel in New Orleans. I gave him $100 and said there would be another $100 bonus if he would meet me after the game. We set a location to meet, and the plan was in place.

So, after the game I sought out Edd Hargett, former A&M quarterback and teammate who was now with the Saints. I told him about my deal with the cabby and he said, "Tommy, it sounds like your marriage depends on catching that 6 p.m. flight. What makes you think that cab driver will meet you? It's like you already paid him!" I hadn't thought of that. Edd said, "Listen, man, Jim Ninowski (QB for the Saints) has a 5:30 flight to catch and he's riding in a police car to get to the airport. You better ride with him."

Okay. Change of plans.

In my naivete, I asked Coach Shula after that game if I could have the upcoming Tuesday off because I was getting married on Monday (this was Sunday—Monday was our off day). Coach looked at me funny and said, "No! You cannot have Tuesday off. Be at practice!" I wasn't sure how that would work out, but I hoped it would—somehow.

What a ride that was in the police car with Jim Ninowski! The police officer turned on his sirens and people were scattering to get out of the way. I started giggling and, with a good ol' Cajun accent, the passenger police officer said, "Heh, mon, let's not be a-loffin' now. You boys are criminals and criminals don't loff on da way to de jail. Okeee?"

We got to the airport about fifteen minutes before my plane took off, and I ran to the counter. Jim ran with me and told the flight folks who he was, saying we had just finished a game. We begged them to hold the plane. This would never happen today with all the security procedures.

I guess the flight attendants waiting at the gate had heard about these goofy football guys. They were grinning ear to ear when we arrived. The plane took off, and sitting in my seat, feeling very thankful, I plugged in to some music. Do you remember the old Academy Award-winning musical *My Fair Lady* and the song, "Get me to the church on time"? That's what was playing in my earphones—no lie!

Growing up in Houston, we had a neighbor, a man named King Cruise, who owned a Cessna dealership. When my plane landed in Houston after the New Orleans game, King had arranged for a pilot to meet me and take me to a smaller plane that would fly me to Brady, Texas that Sunday.

Yup, I made it to Brady, just in time for the wedding rehearsal and dinner afterward. And the wedding happened as planned, Monday, October 20th, 1969, at 7 p.m. at the First Baptist Church.

Of course, by tradition, I never saw Janice on Monday until she came down the aisle. My Baylor Beauty was lookin' good!

The church was packed. I remember smiling a lot and especially the moment we recited our vows to each other. After the ceremony, we greeted everyone in front of the church.

Now this was Brady, Texas and these were country folks. They were a lot more interested in their tractors, animals, and their hometown girl, Janice, than this boy they didn't know. An old rancher gave me a look and said, seriously, "Now, where are you takin' Janice?"

I answered, "Baltimore, Maryland."

He paused, and said, "Now just where is that?"

115

I told him and he said, "Well, boy, that's way out on the East Coast. You are gonna take care of this girl, aren't ya?"

I nodded. "Yes sir, I am."

He knew Janice's family, and he cared for this Brady girl he'd known a lot longer than some football guy.

We got in our rental car and drove to Dallas for a 10 a.m. flight to Baltimore on Tuesday morning.

We were actually supposed to fly from Brady to Houston in the Cessna to catch a 1 a.m. flight to Baltimore. That was the first plan. But I had called earlier to check on the flight and heard some scary news. There was a hurricane developing off the coast and the Houston airports were shut down!

There was no way the Cessna could come get us and no way to catch a 1 a.m. flight to Baltimore. I called the Colts general manager and told him about the hurricane. I told him I couldn't make it back Tuesday. I heard myself say, "Tell Coach I'm gonna miss practice."

CHAPTER 8
SUPER BOWL V

HURRICANE BOY

"No! You cannot have Tuesday off. Be at practice!"

I could see Coach Shula bearing down on me and nearly shouting those words, just a few days earlier. It played over and over in my head. I didn't know what the consequences would be, but I was going to face them. I walked into the team facilities Wednesday morning and on into the locker room.

Players were laughing when they saw me. Tom Matte, whose locker was next to mine (he enjoyed filling my shoes with powder and wrapping all my clothes up with training tape), was the first to say, "Hello, Mr. Hurricane Boy."

Lots of laughter followed that remark. I thought, *What's so funny about that?* I realized that all my teammates thought I had made up the whole story. I tried to convince them there really was a hurricane warning, but it only made them laugh harder. Weather wasn't national news back in those days. But the consequences were just getting started…

Everybody quieted down for the morning meeting. Then,

in front of the whole team, Coach Shula pointed out that one of their teammates, Hurricane Boy, chose to get married on Monday and couldn't get back on Tuesday. Because of a…hurricane (they laughed each time they heard the word hurricane). Coach Shula carefully pointed out that, according to the rules, a fine must be paid for missing practice—regardless of the excuse. Coach Shula said, "You may know by now that we have a newlywed on the team whose new name is Hurricane Boy." Then, he recounted the story, emphasized it was a weak, flimsy excuse, but in this case, he was going to let the players decide the matter. Great.

He asked for a show of hands. Should I be shown some grace for missing practice, considering the marriage and the Hurricane Boy story? No hands went up. All the players remained silent. Most were grinning.

Then coach asked how many of them thought the fine should stand. Without hesitation, every arm in the room shot up. Yep, it was unanimous.

So I got fined, lost some money—but I gained a beautiful wife. In the end, it was easy to see who really won in this game of tease and tackle. You got it. Hurricane Boy.

A LIFE-LONG CALLING

While I was with the Colts, 1969–1971, I was continually exposed to God's Word. Several men on the team helped guide me as a fairly new Christian. One conversation really stands out, talking to a great offensive lineman, Bob Vogel.

After a Bible study, Bob and I somehow ended up sitting in my car. Bob spoke to various high school teams and men's groups, sharing his testimony and his faith in Jesus Christ. He took me with him a couple of times. This time it was just Bob and me.

Out of the blue, he hit me with the question that every pro football player must face. "Tommy, what are you going to do when you can't play football anymore?" As a rookie on the team, I never thought about life after football. Before I could work up an answer, he shot another question. It was almost prophetic, as if God was giving me a glimpse of events to come. "Tommy, every Christian has a ministry. For some it's full time. You need to pray and ask God to lead you into your ministry."

My ministry. That was a callout moment. For the first time, I considered the fact that God might actually have a long-term calling on my life.

SERGEANT MAXWELL

After my first year with the Colts, I served six months of active duty for the Army National Guard in Fort Jackson, South Carolina. The Colts approached me about joining the Guard, mostly because they didn't want to lose me to the regular Army and the Vietnam war. Plus, this was stateside duty, so I could miss weekday meetings to attend football practice. My captain was really a character. He was always wanting me to drive him somewhere, and once in the car, he would give me a running commentary on the game the Colts had just played.

During basic training, we weren't allowed to go home for a couple of months. The first day, our drill sergeant asked my platoon if anyone of us had played football in college. I raised my hand and looked around. I was the only one with his hand in the air. Well, I became the platoon sergeant under the staff sergeant. I had to make sure the whole platoon was up, dressed, and in formation every morning, looking snappy and standing at attention.

Since there were always some rebels who had to be put back in line, I put together a military goon squad of tough guys who made sure everyone was up and in order. And I didn't sleep well in our open barracks since a rumor was going around that some rebels were out to get me. That was another world and made me appreciate the corps at Texas A&M (although I wasn't part of it), which was one-third of the student population at that time.

OFFSEASONS

Janice Maxwell is one busy lady. Always has been.

To stay busy during that first offseason with the Colts, and while I was away at Army boot camp, Janice worked as a speech pathologist, making good use of her master's degree in speech pathology from Baylor University. For the next six years, I stayed on duty with the National Guard, just going to monthly meetings and summer weeklong training camps.

That second offseason, spring of '71, we stayed in Baltimore and I worked as a speaker for the Colts. They would line me up to speak at various service clubs and bar fan clubs called "Colt Corrals." After a few drinks, the blue-collar folks would get pretty rowdy and ask questions like, "Why in the heck did you let Carrol Dale get behind you?" I learned a little about keeping your cool with drunk people.

My third offseason, spring of '72, Janice and I moved to Bryan-College Station. I had a business degree from Texas A&M and really thought I would like to be a doctor. So, I enrolled at A&M and took two courses: organic chemistry and physics. I never thought about using a tutor to get help and so the doctor dream disappeared with average grades in both courses.

That time in Bryan holds some clear memories for me. Our first child, Lezley, was born there. I also remember sitting in physics class with my eyes crossed trying to understand something that the prof was saying. But the Lord had us right where we needed to be.

FIRST STEPS INTO CHURCH LIFE

God put me in a relationship with Pastor Bailey Stone and some of the great folks at the First Baptist church in Bryan, Texas. I had never been baptized or involved in a church since I started my relationship with Jesus that junior year at Texas

A&M. I remember Bailey visiting us in our condo and explaining to me the significance of baptism for someone who had placed their faith in Christ.

Bailey explained that it was a step of obedience which Jesus himself followed to show his relationship with the God of Israel and God's chosen people. And Jesus gave baptism a fuller meaning. It was not just identifying with God and His people, but identifying with God's ultimate plan of salvation for many, all over the world.

Jesus, God's son, took on his shoulders every selfish thought and unkind action that God's people committed every day. The perfect Son of God died a judgment-death for us, a death that we deserved. This perfect payment covered us with his perfection. So now, God sees our hearts of faith, just as he sees his Son. Amazing.

Bailey explained that, by going under the water, baptism symbolizes our dying with Jesus, dying to God's necessary judgment of sin, and dying with Jesus to the power of sin over us. And, symbolically, his children come out of the water as new people, covered with Jesus' perfection, positionally (Galatians 2:20).

Yes, baptism is God's perfect and beautiful illustration of how he sees us in his Son, wrapped in Jesus' perfection. God gives us the faith to believe this by the Holy Spirit. And the Holy Spirit causes us to live wanting to obey God's perfect will. We come alive, so to speak, with a new "want to" attitude, a thankful attitude, and a growing desire to please our Creator. We're not sinless, but we sin less and less.

That offseason, God used Bailey and Joyce Stone to open up a whole new world for Janice and me. We also became close friends with Sam and Janice Wood as neighbors in the same condos. Sam worked as a young pharmacist while his wife, Janice, was a stay-at-home mom. All I can remember is fun and laughter in our relationship. We practically spent every day together.

And, my country girl bride (who admits she kind of likes the smell of horses) loved petting the horses in a field right behind our condo. Those horses were always happy to see us when we brought handfuls of carrots and apples.

That seemed like a quick offseason after my second year of pro football, filled with four warm memories for me: the birth of our daughter, Lezley; becoming close with Bailey and Joyce, and Janice and Sam; Janice and the horses; and finally, my baptism.

I have one other great memory: riding in a 1930 Ford Model A we called "The Doozy." It was a life saver for us because Lezley had some bad colic episodes (lots of crying) and the only thing that seemed to help her was our chuggedy-chug rides in "The Doozy." I guess the sound, and maybe the vibration of the car, knocked her out quickly. And, since there was always a kind of warm, old-time car smell, we wondered if that helped her, too! We used to laugh about it as an afterthought. Lezley would sleep most of the way through all the trips we made.

123

THE BIG ONE: SUPER BOWL V

One of the more memorable experiences in my life—in my entire football career—came on January 17, 1971. I was with the Baltimore Colts when we played the Dallas Cowboys in Super Bowl V. This marked the first Super Bowl since the AFL/NFL merger.

The game started at 2:00 p.m. under the hot Miami sun. The heat was made worse by this being the very first Super Bowl ever played on an artificial surface.

The start time was early. In fact, this was the first Super Bowl played before noon in the Pacific time zone. Despite the early start time, 46.1 million people still tuned in to watch what would later be called the "Blunder Bowl."

The two teams combined for a total of eleven turnovers in this historical game that still stands as the only Super Bowl where a member of the losing team won the MVP. And a defensive MVP at that. The award went to Chuck Howley of the Cowboys.

I remember well a team meeting about halfway through the season before the Super Bowl. We were not sure what to think as the coaches were not invited to this one. We hadn't been playing too well and the older players were still blaming and pointing fingers for the Colts' loss to the Jets in Super Bowl III in 1969. Despite the fact that the Jets were picked to lose by about 20 points, Joe Namath had gone public that the Jets would beat the Colts—and then shocked the world by doing that very thing.

Really, a large number of Colt players carried bad feelings toward Super Bowl III. Now, the night before the big game, they called us to meet right after dinner to address the importance of Super Bowl V.

In that same room, they had makeshift, stadium-style seating for the players. We found our places on the seats. The chatter calmed down and the meeting began. Some of the retiring older players looked at the younger players, telling them this was their last chance to win the Big One. They all had something to say, venting strong feelings about how the Colts screwed up Super Bowl III.

Veteran linebacker Mike Curtis stood up at one point and let it be known, "I'm going to cut right to the chase here, fellas. If we lose, I'm going to kick every single one of your butts."

That was his talk. And we knew he might very well do just that.

UNITAS STANDS UP

The last man to stand up and talk was the great Johnny Unitas.

He had been injured earlier in the year and had very little playing time for a quarterback of his caliber. But he was the unquestioned leader of our team. He was the Arnold Palmer of football at that time.

He stood quietly before the team for an almost awkward

amount of time, looking every player directly in the eyes. Everyone sat stone still and dead silent. Our leader was about to speak and everyone was glued to him, waiting. Nobody dared say a word.

Finally, he broke the silence. "If I hear one word from anyone about that Super Bowl we lost against the Jets, or if you talk about what another player should've done, I'm going to personally kick you off this team. I don't care where we are, at a restaurant, in the locker room, on the field—I'm going to personally kick you off this team."

He meant it. He'd had it with all the negative talk and focus on the past.

Unitas continued. "Fellas, we've been griping and complaining ever since we lost that Super Bowl. But this is what we're going to do. We're going to start encouraging one another. Building one another up. Doing everything we can to make each member of this team a better player. And if we do that, we will win the Super Bowl. You understand?"

After these words, he turned around and walked right out of the room. Our captain's words spoke louder than any pep talk we had ever heard.

We all remained seated in the awkward moment that followed. Nobody knew what to do. Eventually, some of the older players led us out and we heard some of them saying, "I've never heard Johnny give a talk about anything."

He was a quiet leader. When I got back to the hotel room, Rick Volk was jumping from his bed to my bed. I asked, "What are you doing?"

Without stopping his motion, he just started yelling, "We're going to win the Super Bowl!"

And that was how I felt too. Johnny had said it, and he was The Man. We had hope again.

O'BRIEN'S BIG KICK

Game Day. Super Bowl V. Guess I'll skip the play-by-play and get to the amazing part.

With a little over a minute left in the game, tied 13–13, Rookie Colt kicker Jim O'Brien kicked off and the ball went into the end zone.

The Cowboys took it on the 20 yard line. They started their march down the field. 10 yards. 12 yards. 8 yards. They were on the 50 yard line with 15 seconds on the clock.

It was second down and long when Craig Morton rolled right and threw the ball to Dan Reeves, who tipped it up. Mike Curtis, our All-Pro middle linebacker, made a diving interception. And—since Mike was a fullback in college—I guess he thought he could run it back for a TD.

He was trying to bring back the old moves, but they were just not there. He forgot he was now a linebacker! With the clock ticking down 15 seconds, 12 seconds, we were all screaming, "Get down, Mike! Get down!"

We wanted a chance at a field goal, and thankfully the Cowboys took him down on the 32 yard line with 8 seconds left on the clock.

127

Now here's where it gets good. You will have to tune in to the TV when they replay the highlights of past Super Bowls. Then you can give your friends some commentary on Jim O'Brien's Big Kick. Because this is how it happened.

Sam Havrilak and I were friends with Jim, and we thought we should go up and say something to him. He was a young player like Sam and me (only a few "young'uns" like us were on the old Baltimore Colts team), and we wanted to encourage Jim. Not wise.

Best to leave your kicker alone at times like that. Anyway, we meandered up to Jim and said, "How ya doing, Jim?"

He looked at us with that look. "Well, stupid, how do you think I'm doing?" he said, and continued, "Not so good! You don't understand the pressure, man!"

Uh-oh, dumb idea, I thought.

Now here comes the funny part.

Billy Ray Smith, a tough, older defensive player for the Colts, came slowly walking toward us. We were all afraid of Billy Ray since we had heard stories of his ferocious boxing days and how he leveled a guy in Dallas after a mildly offensive exchange.

Let me digress on that encounter so you can know Billy better. Some guy on the freeway in Dallas had flipped Billy Ray off and Billy Ray signaled for him to pull over. The stupid guy pulled over. Well, as the story goes, they met outside a hotel right off Central Expressway. Then, BOOM! Billy Ray gut punched him before he knew what happened. The guy went down—gasping for air. Anyway, Billy Ray called the police and stayed there until they came. He could be nice like that...to his

128

victims.

Now to continue. On this hot day in Miami, Billy Ray came walking toward Jim, Sam, and myself, with a very serious and tired look on his face. Sam and I froze in place. Billy Ray grabbed Jim O'Brien by his shoulder pads, put his facemask right on Jim's, and said, "Son, there's millions of bucks riding on this kick. Now you go make it!"

Billy gave Jim a big shove and the young player stumbled forward, staggering onto the field.

Jim got his footing, then turned around and chuckled. There we were, witnessing the old NFL in action without realizing it. Folks, you would never see anything like that today.

Well, the Cowboys called time-out to give Jim some time to think about his chance to win the Super Bowl. But what they didn't know was that Jim was already locked in. He could have waited all day because his mind was made up. Make it or face Billy Ray! Easy choice.

Jim kicked it so perfectly, it could have been a 60-yard field goal. He put it right through the middle. And—here is the best part:

Sam Havrilak came up to me after all the celebration and said, "Hey, Tommy, I didn't realize that Billy Ray was such a great psychologist!"

I will always remember that line. Almost fifty years later, I still laugh when I do.

Scan this QR code for Tommy's sports videos and interviews.

CHAPTER 9
OAKLAND RAIDER #42

MADDEN CALLS

The joy of winning the Super Bowl with the Colts was short-lived. A few months after the game, Janice and I were staying with her folks in Brady, Texas.

Her mom tapped on the door of our room about midnight and said that there was a Mr. John Madden on the phone. Barely awake, wondering who the heck John Madden was, I picked up the phone to hear a voice that would become very familiar over the next few years.

Oakland Raiders coach John Madden said, "Tommy, we are excited to have you as part of our organization."

I didn't know what to say. Another awkward silence.

Coach Madden continued. "Tommy, have the Colts not contacted you about our trade?"

"No sir," I mumbled.

Coach Madden said a few choice words and then told me he was glad I was a Raider and that he would have the Colts contact me first thing.

To this day, I still don't know how the Raiders found me in Brady, but as a fan of Raider history, I know they could always find a way.

I was surprised, to say the least, as I still considered myself a Colt. I mean, we had just won the Super Bowl title—the first in the modern era with the merger of two major American football leagues, the NFL and the AFL.

As I climbed in bed staring at the ceiling, I remember thinking, "Well, if you're going to be traded, it's nice to be traded to another team who may also reach the Super Bowl."

THE NOTORIOUS RAIDERS

I had to process it. The year was 1971 and I'd just been traded to the notorious Oakland Raiders. A team known for being "the bad boys" of pro football. A team that would, in the upcoming years, lead me all the way to…growing sideburns! I learned pretty quickly that the team in Oakland was a family that lived by the motto, "Once a Raider, always a Raider." To this day, I still get gifts and birthday cards from the Raiders organization.

Back then, at the end of training camp, they had a kind of bowling tournament for those who made the 40-man squad (team roster). I remember a manager coming up to me toward the end of training camp my first year with the Raiders and announcing that I was "Billy Bob's" (well-known Raider, not his real name) partner in this bowling tournament. He then told me

132

to go to this local bar for the tournament.

Hmmm. A bar for bowling? Interesting. Well, when I walked in, the place was hoppin'! Lots of excitement in the air. Then I saw what kind of bowling tournament this was. Remember the arcade-style bowling games? You stood at the miniature alley, about 10 feet long by 2 feet wide, which was raised up on four legs, and you pushed a small puck to hit the automated pins at the far end. When you hit the pins, they'd flip up into the machine. That kind of bowling.

Billy Bob came up and leaned on me. With somewhat slurred, happy hour language, he said, "Taammmmy (that's me, Tommy), I've been a Raider for 10 (hiccup) years and have never won this towwmaah-ment (tournament). I don't bow-wwwl that well (burp) and you have to come through, man. You got ta carrrry us, man. You can dooo thisss, man."

I looked at him and said, "I have never done this before, Billy Bob, but I'll give it a try."

Maybe since I was the only sober one in the whole bar, I started rolling strikes. Honestly, I think the machine was broken. Anyway, we won the tournament and Billy Bob was the happiest man I have ever seen in my life. That seemed very strange at the time, but not so strange as you get to know the Raiders—back then, anyway. He actually had tears in his eyes.

Now this is the part you will not believe, but it gives you a little insight into a rather unique football team. Before I knew it, big hands under my legs carried me and Billy Bob around the bar. Champaign corks popped and champagne sprayed. Billy Bob and I were soaked. Very different from the Super Bowl victory I had celebrated just six months prior!

Janice still remembers me calling her that night and saying, "I'm not sure what planet I've landed on, but it's in the Raider Galaxy for sure."

Yeah, this was a different brand of football than I was used to. But, you know what? It was fun.

The club president and part owner was Al Davis. What a character—but a fun and very smart character. He knew the business side and had a nose for talent, as well as understood the strategy of the game. That made him a very interesting man since he was not an athlete and never part of any athletic team.

If you asked Al how he knew something, he would always say, "I know everything!"

And, I think he did. I used to laugh at that statement. Yet, at a reunion dinner in honor of George Blanda, who had passed away, Al gave a fascinating history of AFL football (which he helped start). It should have been recorded. That would have been the best TV football special ever. And it all happened under the old Raider stadium. They had set up tables with about eight former players around each table. What an evening!

BLANDA & MADDEN

My first meeting with Raider legend George Blanda was typical Blanda.

It had roots going back to my Baby Oiler days, when I met many players, one being Oakland Raider legend George Blanda, who went on to play until he was 48 years old.

As an adult, at my first Raider workout, I went up and introduced myself to George. I said, "You may not remember me, but when I was a Baby Oiler, 13 years old, I met you. We played an inter-squad game at halftime during an Oiler game. You shook the team's hands after our performance."

He looked at me for a second and said, "You little…I knew if I stayed around this game long enough, one of you little…would get old enough to play with me."

Typical Blanda.

George used to enjoy talking about his Houston Oiler heydays and I would egg him on, since I asked a lot of questions about players and games. George Blanda and John Madden were really the faces of the franchise at that time and both had unique personalities. They and Al Davis gave the Raiders their well-earned reputation.

Coach Madden was a different kind of coach. He had an easy smile, a refreshing honesty, and a creativity that you don't see in many coaches. None of us were surprised to see what a great commentator Coach Madden later became on TV. He made it personal with individual players and offered insights, not only into their skills, but also into their personalities. He actually enjoyed the different personalities of each player as much as their football ability.

He wouldn't just say, "nice block" as a normal TV commentator might say when describing a certain play; he would talk about the quirks of the player and describe why it was a nice block. He truly loved the game of football and liked to hang out with the players, especially offensive linemen, since that was his old position.

Now Coach Madden liked psychology. I heard that was his major in college. I remember a couple of funny times when he would bring out his psychology insights to enlighten us.

One time, we played the Cowboys in a preseason game in Dallas. It was the first time we had played in their new stadium, which had synthetic turf. It was a thin, rug-like material called Tartan Turf, laid over an asphalt surface—very hard. The players all talked about the hard field, stepping on it, pressing it with their fingers.

Coach Madden walked up and delivered a typical Madden psychology lecture. He said, "What do you guys think about this turf?"

One of the players said what we were all thinking. "Coach, this stuff is hard. I feel like we're playing on cement."

Then Coach Madden jumped on that. "You just think it's hard. It's not really hard."

Okay. We all knew that a psychology lesson was coming. Coach Madden loved these get-into-your-head moments. "Listen guys, the cushioning under this material is like the cushioning on the dashboard of a car. When you feel the dashboard of a car, it feels hard, right? But, if you have an accident and slam into the dashboard, it gives with you, right? That's what happens when you run or fall on this field."

One of the players sarcastically said, "Wow, Coach, that was fascinating. Why don't you run and take a jump in the air and land your body on this stuff to show us how it gives with you?"

Madden actually liked that kind of kidding. As I recall, one of the players giggled and Madden had to smile too. I think he realized that it was a strange conversation before a football game, but that's what made Coach Madden kind of lovable. He was not like the grim-faced, no-nonsense coaches you may have had. Madden always wanted to pass along some new revelation. He was always philosophizing because everything was always about the mind—and positive thinking. And, get this, he wanted us to call him "John," not "Coach."

My friend Monte Johnson has a great Madden story. Monte, a second round draft pick from Nebraska, was selected as a middle linebacker. "I was fortunate to play for John Madden," Monte told me. "He was as much a teacher about life as a great football coach. One year, I was injured in a game against the Broncos, and it didn't look like I'd be able to play the next week. Sure enough, in the locker room, I overheard teammates saying Ted would start for me. I was not happy. In his office, John confirmed it. Ted was starting for me. In a rage, I stood up, kicked away the chair and stormed out. John, in a calm voice, said, 'Monte, get back in here, and if you don't, it's going to cost you $5,000 for every minute you don't.' I walked back in, set the chair, and sat down. He asked if I had a quarter. I did. He asked me to hold it up and said, 'What do you see?' I described my side of the quarter. He said that's not what he saw on his side. Then I realized—this wasn't about quarters. It was about how you look at life. John's point was that there are two sides to every situation. When you learn to see things from another person's point of view, it helps you as a leader—and helps you not make a fool of yourself! The end of the story? Ted did start for me, but then John put me back in! 'I told Ted he was going to start for you,' Madden later said, 'not play the whole game.' I can't look at a quarter without thinking of that life lesson from John Madden."

Monte went on to become a successful businessman and a Bible Study Fellowship leader in Atlanta, Georgia.

Here's another Coach Madden story. On an unusually hot and humid day in Oakland, during practice, Coach Madden heard some of the players complaining about the heat. Of course, being a Houston, Texas boy, I knew hot and humid, and it was not that bad. Of course, Madden being Madden, a fix-all psychology lecture was on the way.

He gathered us together. "Boys, it is not that hot! You're used to a cooler climate in California. You just have to tell your brain that it's not that hot. Just keep saying to yourself, 'It feels cool today. It sure feels cool,' and you'll forget about the temperature. Stop talking about it being hot!"

Well, he was lecturing to players decked out in complete uniforms, and he had on a Raiders T-shirt and Bermuda shorts.

About halfway through practice, Coach Madden became dizzy, took a knee, and the trainer ran in his direction with some ice. Coach Madden was a big man. We were concerned, but some of the players were kidding with each other, saying, "It's not that hot," as they saw the trainer putting ice on Coach Madden.

As he became more conscious, we could see that smile come across his face. Coach Madden could laugh at himself, and he did. He looked up at the players and said, "Well, maybe it is hot. Practice is over."

I miss Coach Madden.

CHAPTER 10
NOT SO FAST

THE NICKNAME

Most of the Raiders had a nickname.

You knew you had arrived if you had a nickname.

I didn't have one. Not yet.

Fridays were called easy days because it was mostly film-watching and a short review on the field. At one point during practice, Coach Madden would stand on the sideline and call out special teams so each man knew his position (kickoff team, field goal team, punt team, etc.).

Eventually, it was time for the onside kickoff return team to hit the field, and I was part of it. In fact, I had a somewhat prestigious position since I was in the middle of the left side where the right-footed kickers would try to send a wobbly kick toward you. You were thought to have "good hands" if you were put on the front line of an onside kickoff return team.

Well, for two games in a row, I had onside kicks come right to me. You hardly ever see onside kicks—so that was rare. The first game, I bobbled the kick and it went out of bounds. The second one in the next game, I bobbled, but also recovered.

The next Friday practice after that second bobble, Coach Madden called for the onside kickoff return team to come to the practice field. As usual, I ran to "my" position. You know, the position (I thought) I deserved.

When I lined up, Coach Madden stood close to me and called out, "Maxwell!"

That caught my attention. "We're putting Bob at your position."

That was embarrassing! I wanted to protest. Or at least ask if we could talk about it. But in pro ball, your feelings don't really matter. Performance matters. After two bobbles, Coach wanted a reliable, experienced player there.

Then, the perennial All-Pro guard, Gene Upshaw, took the opportunity to holler out, loud and clear for everyone to hear it:

"NOT SO FAST, MAXWELL!"

Well, you already know the rest of the story. Yep, Not So Fast became yours truly. Not the nickname I would have picked, but I'm not in control of things, am I?

Upshaw had noticed that I trotted over to the position I thought was mine. But things change—players rotate—he'd probably seen that kind of thing before. I'm sure I looked like a sorry pup, walking away from "my place" on a special team.

And, unfortunately—or maybe fortunately—the name

stuck. In fact, about six years ago, a friend of mine ran into Phil Villapiano (great linebacker for Oakland, nicknamed "Foo") and asked him if he knew me. Phil smiled and said, "Sure, I know ol' Not So Fast." As time has moved on, I actually enjoy telling the story behind the nickname.

So, the Not So Fast story continued to spread. To honor George after his passing, the Raiders family contacted all the former Raiders who had played with George Blanda to attend a reunion in Oakland. They paid for everything. Al Davis loved George, and George won many a game for the Raiders as a field goal kicker—very unusual for a quarterback.

What a special reunion. It brought back so many memories. At a reception in the hotel, many past and present Raiders came together. An active Raider came up to me and said, "So, you're Not So Fast. I didn't think I'd get a chance to meet you."

He went on, "We had a get together party not too long ago and voted for the best nicknames of all time."

He looked at me and smiled. "Did you know that you were the number one pick?"

I thanked him and later got to thinking…I never was a starter with the Raiders. I was always frustrated and half-mad about that, but some of my best stories have come from being on that team.

I wish I could have enjoyed myself more because it was a rare group of fun guys and great football players. We should have won the Super Bowl every year I was there, but we just couldn't get there, even though we were always in the playoffs.

Not long ago, I complained to a friend about how I wish

I'd been a starter for the Raiders, even though I was a fifth defensive back and came in frequently on third and long passing downs.

We would man-to-man all the potential receivers. My friend did a little research and said, "Tommy, did you know that all the defensive backs from your days with the Raiders are now All-Pro—including two who are in the Pro Football Hall of Fame?"

I did get to be the upback on punt returns. I would position about 10 yards in front of George Atkinson and catch the shorter punts. George was a good return man, and he would call out, "You got it, Maxwell!" on shorter punts. So, I mostly fair caught the shorter, more difficult punts.

The Raiders were known to play, well, a little more than just aggressively. Some would say they played dirty. I wasn't really accepted until a couple of incidences. Then, unknowingly, a chance came to become a truly accepted Raider!

We were playing the Los Angeles Rams. I had to come across the line to turn back a sweep play. In those situations, you will always have a 275-pound pulling guard barreling towards you with a smile on his face. I'm not kidding. They were always smiling—very intimidating. You have to either go into a self-defense mode and stand your ground, or turn and start running away (a temptation), which would look somewhat cowardly.

It all happened very quickly, but I remember doing the only thing that could possibly stop this killer's attack on my poor body. I popped his helmet with the palm of my hand and he

144

went down like a 100-pound bag of corn and didn't even move for a good five minutes. I never knew what happened since I tried to make a play on the runner. When I came to the huddle after the play was over, all the secondary players were excitedly saying, "Maxwell, you killed that boy over there! You killed him, man!"

I said, "You're crazy!"

They persisted. "Look at him, Maxwell, he's just layin' there, man. He's dead! I'm tellin' ya—he's dead!"

I kept looking over. And he just kept laying there. I began to worry. Finally, LA's trainer and crew helped lift him up and he staggered off the field. Well, I became a true Raider that night, fully accepted as one of the Raider "bad boys."

The most frustrating year was when we lost the AFC division playoff against the Pittsburgh Steelers in the famous Immaculate Reception game. Google it for more info. I'll just say this: No one said a word on the plane ride all the way home. Scan this QR code for Tommy's sports videos and interviews.

BACK HOME: HOUSTON OILERS

My career came full circle in 1974 when I signed with the Houston Oilers.

I started as a KILT Baby Oiler and would end my career playing in my hometown for the professional Oilers. I was with the Oilers for one season when I started having neck pain. A team doctor ran tests and the result was not good. More on that later.

By far the best memory from that time is my relationship with Oail Andrew Phillips, Jr., football player, United States Marine, executive, and coach. Known to pretty much everybody as "Bum" Phillips.

Later in life, as executive director of Coaches Outreach (CO), I called Coach Phillips to ask him if he would speak for our annual CO dinner. I was surprised that he answered the phone at his home in Texas. I briefly told him about our ministry to coaches. He said, "Let me get Debbie on the phone; she loves Bible studies."

Bum's wife, Debbie, came to the phone and I described our ministry to her. She listened politely to my description of Coaches Outreach and then shared how Coach Phillips recently had heart bypass surgery, and she was trying to keep him rested.

Bum was still on the phone and said, "Debbie!"

She responded, "Yes, Bum?"

"I'm not dead yet!" He boomed. "I'd like to go talk for that banquet."

She responded, "Okay, Bum, I'll drive you."

Still makes me smile. So, at their invitation, Janice and I went to visit Coach Phillips at his ranch.

As we pulled in, four dogs rushed out of the house and ran up to the car. Debbie invited us in and told us that Bum was out riding on his tractor. "That man loves his tractor more than me," she said.

I was looking around in Bum's somewhat small, typical country house, when Debbie asked to be excused for a minute. She went away and came back to find me looking at football stuff. "Looking for football paraphernalia?" she asked.

I gave her a "Yes, ma'am," in response.

She said, "Well, Bum has given it all away for fundraisers and it's all gone."

Then Coach Phillips walked into the house with a big smile. Tractor rides did it for him!

Janice, Debbie, and I went outside with Coach Phillips to their covered indoor arena. His ranch hand was trying to put a new leveling dragger on Bum's tractor. Debbie was giving instructions, but he ignored her. Finally, she had enough and couldn't hold back. "Do you think women are dumb?" she said, intense—but under control. "Get out of my way and I'll show both you and Bum how to put this thing on!"

Like that, she hooked it up, which took some real know-how! Yep, Debbie is a real country lady.

Later on, we had lunch in Goliad, at the little café on the square. People passed by, saying howdy to Bum and Debbie. We picked up some feed at the local feed store, and that afternoon went to their round horse pen where Debbie was showing a girl how to train her cutting horse. Bum was proud to tell us that he and a friend had built the horse pen.

What a perfect Texas setting it was on that warm spring afternoon. We sat on the upper stands above that arena, watching those muscled, athletic horses do their magic—cutting out one cow and keeping her from going back to the herd. What a

147

sheer joy for me and my small town, horse-lovin' wife, Janice.

I looked over at Bum, sitting there with his arms folded. From the hat to the boots, he was a portrait of perfect contentment. I just had to say, "Coach, you sure look happy."

He looked back at me and said, "Tommy boy, who wouldn't be? Everything I love and need is right here."

He looked out with those satisfied eyes, gazing at his surroundings. It was one of those moments you think, "God's in his heaven and all's right with the world."

One more Bum Phillips story, costarring Pastor Chuck Swindoll.

Several years later, at a Coaches Outreach Saturday night banquet, after Coach Phillips spoke, he mentioned to me how much he loved hearing Chuck Swindoll on radio and really wanted to visit his church. He was kind of insistent about it, in his friendly way.

So, the next day, I drove us out to Stonebriar Community Church in North Dallas. Since I had worked for Chuck when he was president of Dallas Theological Seminary, I looked forward to seeing him again.

I knew Chuck had a habit of greeting as many people as he could before church started, so we got there early. We waited in line and then Chuck turned to see Coach Phillips. This is one football-loving pastor and his eyes lit up with excitement to see Bum Phillips right there, standing in line. Chuck reached out and heartily shook hands with Bum. Then he exclaimed, as if reaching the final point in a sermon, "You are my coach! Bum Phillips!" I should explain, Chuck Swindoll was from Houston, so he really felt like Bum was his coach.

But this nationally known pastor was still standing there in disbelief. He asked, still smiling, "So, Bum, what brings you here to Stonebriar?" Chuck was so excited. It was fun to watch.

"Come to hear you preach," Bum answered, "I listen to you on the radio!" Simple as that.

After we had found our seats and settled in, Chuck stepped into the pulpit. He introduced Bum's presence in the service by saying, "You know I'm no respecter of persons. If the president of the United States showed up at our church, I would not introduce him; I would treat him like any other person—which he is. But today, someone is here, someone very important, right here at Stonebriar Community Church…my coach, Bum Phillips, is our special guest today."

Only Chuck Swindoll, who many call "America's Pastor," could pull that off.

Chuck got into his sermon. I looked at Bum sitting next to me, smiling, enjoying Chuck's voice—in person—and the message, all happening right there in front of him (not just on radio). He was wearing that same look of perfect contentment I saw in his face when we visited his ranch.

I thought, *this is why he is a beloved Texas coach and means so much to so many people.* I truly miss Coach Phillips, and having that day at the Phillips' ranch is a very special memory.

HOME LIFE

God's providence was at work when, in the offseason of 1974 (January–June), we purchased our first home in Bryan, Texas. It was a picture-perfect traditional home. We loved it. It even had a pool.

We became super involved at the First Baptist church in Bryan and became even closer to our pastor and his wife, Bailey and Joyce Stone. We were also good friends with Charlie and Doy McDaniel and David and Melina Schellenberger.

Our daughters, Lauren and Lezley, were just two and four when we moved there.

Lauren had been born the previous year while we were living in Houston. She loved excitement and fun just like her dad. She changed her clothes at least ten times a day, and then checked the mirror to see how she looked in various outfits. Some of them were from Momma's closet, but size made no difference. She kept us laughing.

Lauren was really kind of quiet and didn't talk much. Janice was teaching Lezley Bible verses and Lauren, at around three years old, would just listen. One day, Lezley tried to recite a rather long verse. Lauren jumped in and gave us the whole verse. We couldn't believe it. Miss Very Quiet was listening, just not talking.

I remember snuggling up with the girls on my lap on Saturday mornings, watching cartoons on TV. In our back den was a gas stove and my oversized foam chair, which was the perfect snuggle place. After cartoons, we would go to a local park and do all the activities from swinging to climbing the monkey bars. That was when we started the tradition of donuts on Saturday mornings, which both of the girls have carried into their families to this day.

One thing's for sure about life. It's always changing. Although this was a happy time in our lives, things were about to change. I was about to transition out of football, and into the next season the Lord had for us.

CHAPTER 11
LIFE AFTER FOOTBALL

LOST PUP

After being cut by the Oilers in 1974, I felt like a lost pup.

I received calls from a couple of pro teams and since the World Football League was starting up, I received a couple of calls from coaches and team management. I also got a call from Jack Take-Your-Head-Off Pardee who was now head coach of a new World League team. They lost interest when I told them what I needed salary-wise. $28,000 was too much back then! I would have loved playing for Coach Pardee. He went on to be a great coach. His players had huge respect for him...if he didn't knock their head off their bodies. Just kidding.

The truth is, God had other plans.

There was an older gentleman from our church in Bryan who was a retired seminary professor. I really appreciated this man and the interest he took in me. Again, God brought a Bible coach to spur me along. He taught Greek in seminary and would later help me learn the Greek alphabet. I decided to take him to an A&M game and, helping him make his way up the steps, we got to our seats and settled in for the game.

Well, a man named Bob Walker was sitting nearby. He happened to ask someone who I was. The next week, I received a call from Bob and he asked if I would come to his office at Texas A&M. I don't remember if he told me his position or the reason he wanted to talk, but I said yes. Since I had lost my desire to play any more pro ball, I'd been praying for God to point me in a new direction. I'd heard from other veterans that I would know when it was time to retire, and I had a strong sense it was my time.

For one thing, I had a bad injury that left my neck in a vulnerable position, with bone spurs that could lead to paralysis. That was our team doctor's report, and it helped to explain the tingling I had in my fingers.

A second thing was the whole defensive back situation that continued to wear on me. I didn't like being average at that. And, on top of that, it was hard to face the fact that I would likely never be a starter.

So, I remember meeting Bob Walker and thinking, "This guy is really warm and friendly." I felt a connection to him right away. As I would learn, that was part of what made him such a great development man (fundraiser). And there we sat in his office, making chitchat and then getting to why he wanted to talk to me.

He said he'd watched me handle the older gentleman at the football game and that prompted him to find out more about me. He explained his work for A&M and told me about his search for a field rep who could go and talk with Aggies (many of whom would be older gentlemen), discussing different scholarships to which they could contribute.

He saw how I cared for the man at the game and knew I had a heart and respect for older men—which I always have had for some reason. Bob explained that my position would not be a high-pressure dealmaker, but more like relationship building with an opportunity presented, rather than a direct "ask" for money. Well, I felt I could learn a lot from Bob Walker, and I did. He loved people and also loved to raise money for a great cause. We hit it off and, after talking it over with Janice, it seemed a good fit for me.

Did God put me at that football game, prompting Bob Walker to ask about me? If you believe that there are no coincidences, as I do, then you see all of this as part of God's sovereign plan. The insights that Bob taught me were exactly what I needed to start Coaches Outreach. God was either in control of all this or he was not. He was. And he is!

BLESSED IN BRYAN

Our four years living in Bryan were fun and productive.

A real blessing.

We loved our church and Pastor Bailey Stone, and his wife, Joyce. R.C. Slocum was an assistant football coach at A&M, then later head football coach there. Bailey would come out and run pass patterns while I covered him and R.C. threw him passes. R.C. also went to Bailey's church, and we both loved our pastor.

Bailey would try and put some moves on me, hoping to fake me out. He looked so funny trying that! R.C. and I would crack up. We kidded him not to leave his day job as a preacher.

God put Bailey in my life. He was fun, but his passion and love for a sovereign God were so real. He took time to meet with about five of us young guys in the church. He took us through a special discipleship course where we could ask questions and talk about the basics of the Christian faith. Bailey was God's man in my life, and the group interaction was so edifying and stimulating. Just what I needed.

We had a real close group of friends in Bryan-College Station. We learned what life with small children was all about. We had a nice home with a pool and loved all our friends coming over, swimming, and barbecuing—all the time. Janice and I both have warm memories of these special friends.

One of the friends, David Shellenberger, had a connection with Don Anderson, a traveling Bible teacher. Don would teach several times each week at homes and hotels in different towns. David invited him to come teach our group of friends, and later Don stayed at our house when he came to Bryan. Our study grew to around 15 couples, and if you do the math, that's 30 people, so we asked a local hotel and they let us meet in a large conference room. This definitely was the Lord's work, causing these important connections to occur. Men plan, but God directs all plans. As the Word of God says, "The heart of a man plans his way, but the LORD establishes his steps" (Proverbs 16:9).

Here's the thing about Don Anderson. He loved teaching the Bible and could make it come alive like Prof Smith. Don came into my life when I hungered for a deeper understanding of Scripture.

Also at that time, I had a Bible study with some football players at A&M. Don and I, now friends, would sometimes go jogging at the college. That's when I started asking him, "Where did you go to seminary?" "Why?" "What did you learn?" Yep, I asked a lot of questions.

Don met me once in Dallas where he arranged a meeting with two professors at Dallas Theological Seminary, Dr. Howard Hendricks and Dr. Don Campbell. I really liked them both. Little did I know that they were both legends in the Christian faith and would help to clarify and strengthen my foundational understanding of Scripture.

PLANTING THE SEED FOR SEMINARY

I suppose my desire to go to seminary started back when I played with the Baltimore Colts, from 1969 to 1970. The Colts had a Friday night Bible study with Captain Bill Lewis (former Navy veteran) who lived close to Annapolis, Maryland and the Naval Academy. That was about 50 miles from Baltimore, and he made the drive to meet with us on Friday nights.

Friday night was normally party night in pro football because preparations were over, and Saturdays we would travel to away games or check into a local hotel about 6 p.m. for short meetings and bed checks.

Captain Bill was a really interesting Bible teacher, and that was the first time I'd really looked around in the Bible. You know, there are certain books and passages you tend to go to, but you know other books and other places deserve your attention. Thanks to Bill Lewis, I took a wider look into God's Word. With Captain Bill, it was like diving into an ocean of discovery.

When I was traded to the Oakland Raiders, I really didn't have the Bible teaching or mentoring I had with the Colts. Bob Vogel, All-Pro lineman with the Colts, was a great mentor. He took me with him when he spoke to Christian organizations and challenged me to start asking God to use me the same way.

A common saying in football when you were getting ready to face a tough opposing team was, "You better button your chin strap." Well, when you ask God to use you, and you mean it, you better button your chin strap! The more I spoke to people, the hungrier I became to understand the Bible better. That desire grew, and when I finished my career in football, we settled in Bryan-College Station, the home of my alma mater, Texas A&M.

That's when we rejoined the Baptist church there since, as I said, Janice and I loved Pastor Bailey Stone and his wife, Joyce. Janice attended a study Joyce led for young wives. About five young guys asked Bailey if he would meet with us every week to talk about issues like prayer, Bible verse memory, witnessing, etc. We were all hungry to better understand what the Lord had for us.

His teaching was very practical and the five or six guys involved have all gone on to serve Christ in different ways. As a result of all the ways God has used the men from that group, I'm sure Bailey has received heavenly rewards he never imagined. Bailey shares in the same rewards we do. That's how discipleship works in God's kingdom: "...and what you have heard from me in the presence of many witnesses entrust to faithful men, who will be able to teach others also" (2 Timothy 2:2).

Timothy spent many years in close association with the apostle Paul. He heard divine truth that God had revealed to Paul, who revealed that truth to many other faithful believers (Silas, Barnabus, Luke, etc.). Every Christian should be sharing, with passion, how the truth of God has strengthened their lives. Hey, that's why I wrote this book.

So, as a result of interaction with these Bible teachers, and my visit to Dallas Theological Seminary with Don Anderson, God began planting something...like a seed, ready to sprout. But still, I wasn't sure if I should attend DTS or another seminary. After more conversations, and after seeking God's will, I made my choice.

The Maxwell family, Christmas 1955
Nancy, Kay, and Tommy with parents, Tom Sr. and
Mary. Houston, Texas.

The Breckenridge family, Janice and Joan, with parents
Mildred and Breck.

Played two years for the Baby Oilers during my Junior High years.

All-City footballer, Jesse Jones High School. Also competed in basketball, baseball, swimming, and track.

OUTSTANDING TEAM AWARDS

Van Brown *Most Valuable Back*
George Cox *Most Valuable Lineman*
Tommy Maxwell *Most Improved Player*
Larry Turner *Highest Grade Average*

Most Improved Player,
Outstanding Team Award

Jones Falcons All-City Defense
and 2nd Team Offense

Tommy Maxwell, number 44 in white jersey,
Houston's Post All-City Football Team, 1964.

Battling for a starting position as offensive split-end,
Texas A&M, September 1966

Tutoring with Bobby Joe Conrad, right, pass-catching expert for the St. Louis Cardinals, '66-67, with Coach Gene Stallings

MAXWELL TUTORED
. . . Texas Aggie end Tommy Maxwell is given instructions by Bobby Joe Conrad, right, St. Louis Cardinals star receiver, and head coach Gene Stallings.

Maxwell, 81, with an interception against Baylor Bears, 1967

Interception against the University of Texas, and the first year
A&M beat Texas in 10 years!

I ran track my Junior
Year at A&M. What
do you mean, "Not
So Fast?"

The Sporting News 1968 ALL-AMERICA FOOTBALL TEAM

CHRISTMAS REWARD FOR LITTLE AGGIE FAN
Blain Hart, 10, son of Mr. and Mrs. Charles Hart of 3401 Parkway Terrace, accepts an autographed football from Senior Letterman Tommy Maxwell, right. Looking on were senior lettermen Bob Long, Curley Hallman, and Steve O'Neal. Blain, a diabetic, plans to play football during his college career at A&M.

Presenting an autographed football to 10-year old Blain Hart, Christmas, 1968.

All-American Football Team, 1968

This catch came right after I had intercepted a pass to set it up. Rice Coach Bo Hagan said, "I'll never forget #81. He made the interception right in front of our bench!" November, 1967

Janice and me at a picnic
in Cameron Park, Waco,
Spring 1969

Interception against Alabama at the
Cotton Bowl, 1968

A&M'S TOMMY MAXWELL SETS UP FIRST AG TD
Maxwell Steals a Ken Stabler Pass At Alabama 30
—UPI Telephoto

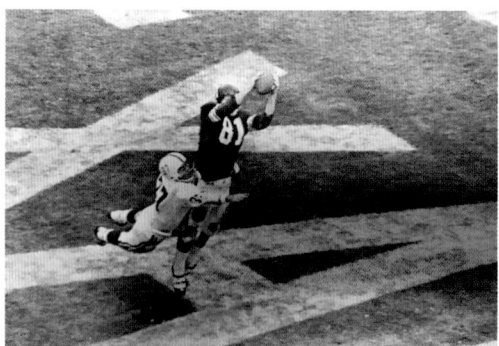

Touchdown catch to put
A&M ahead of Alabama
toward their victory at
the Cotton Bowl, 1968

Publicity photos as #81 at Texas A&M University

Publicity photos as #81
at Texas A&M University

Texas A&M Receivers, Kyle Field, 1967

With our daughters Lezley and Lauren, and my dad, Tom, at the induction ceremony for the A&M Hall of Fame, November 1991.

Janice and I at the A&M Hall of Fame. The plaque is at my right shoulder.

Senior year at A&M. Hall of Fame plaque.

Wedding Day, Monday, October 20, 1968. Coach Shula expected me
back for practice on Tuesday Morning!

PRO CAMP BOUND—Tommy Maxwell, former Texas
A&M star, has been working out here the past few days in
preparation for the Baltimore Colts' summer camp in Westminister, Md. Maxwell is married to the former Janice Breckenridge, daughter of Mr. and Mrs. M. G. Breckenridge.

TOM MAXWELL
Baltimore Colts   DB   6-2   195   Texas A&M

Working out prior to reporting
to the Baltimore Colts, at a
summer camp in Westminister,
Maryland, 1970

Photo for Janice's grandparents,
Mimmie and Aubrey. I loved
them both as my own.

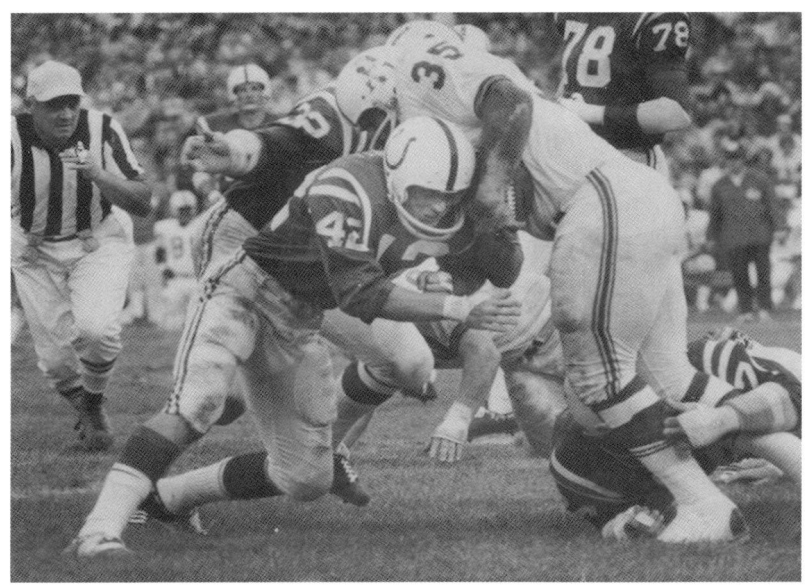

Up against Boston Patriots' Jim Nance, whose leg was bigger than my
body. Don't just stand there, Bubba (Smith), help the boy!

Jerry Don Logan, Earl Morral, and me celebrating Jim
O'Brien's last second victory goal.

All smiles, celebrating at the Post Super Bowl victory party, 1970

During the off-seasons in my NFL Days, encouraging young men in
their faith. Keith Chancey, to my immediate left, is co-founder of
the Kanakuk Institute.

When you watch the Super Bowl, realize the players are thinking about one thing: this ring!

Helmet with signatures of the Super Bowl V Champion
Baltimore Colts

Growing up watching cowboys "bull-dogging" steers came in handy against big ol' running backs. "Can you slow down a little bit?

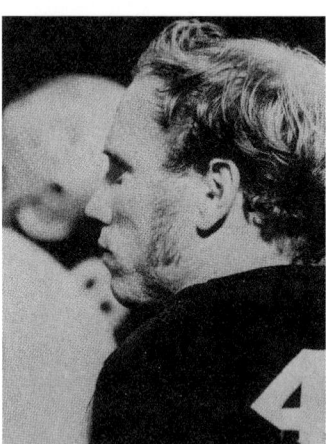

I tried to grow some scruffy-looking sideburns to at least look like a "bad boy" Raider.

Southern boys like me don't like cold games. Tackling running backs seems to hurt more when you're cold.

I kept the #42 with three pro teams: Colts, Raiders, and Oilers.

Proof that pro football players do smile for promotion shots!

Raiders helmet signed by my teammates.

TOMMY MAXWELL   DEFENSIVE BACK

OILERS

From Baby Oiler to Pro Oiler

Our daughter Lezley attends an Oilers/Cowboy game two weeks prior to the arrival of her baby sister, Lauren. 1974

Oilers Kevin Hunt, Ron Saul, Jeff Severson, Zeke Moore, and me presenting an autographed ball to Jose Arita. A young man from Honduras facing leukemia.

Visiting Janice's hometown, Brady, Texas, with Lezley and Lauren. Always fun for this "city boy."

Graduation day: accepting my diploma from Dr. John Walvoord, President of Dallas Theological Seminary, 1973.

This 1930 Ford, "The Doozy," was the second love of my life. Wish I still had it.

Coach Stallings and me, thankful he didn't have me rolling across the floor. 2005

The very first Coaches Outreach Bible Study. Next to me is Head Coach Barry Morgan at Trinity Christian Academy with two of his assistants, around 1988.

One of the first training sessions for Coaches Outreach Lay
Leaders, around 1997

Tommy with little Lauren

Our family: Back Row: Lilly (granddaughter), Nolan (grandson), John (son-in-law), Lauren (daughter), Patrick (son-in-law), Marshall (grandson), Lezley (daughter), Front Row: Maxwell (grandson), Tommy, Janice, Ford (grandson), and Kate (granddaughter).

CHAPTER 12
SEMINARY: A NEW EXPERIENCE

FISH OUT OF WATER

In the fall of 1978, I became a student at Dallas Theological Seminary. Now this was a whole new experience. Maxwell, the fish out of water. I had never studied so hard. There were constant argument papers you had to write, dealing with the "problem passages" in the Bible. My sweet wife would stay up, long after the girls had gone to sleep, typing papers for me. That was after Janice spent all day working as a speech pathologist.

Then there were Greek and Hebrew classes because, as you may know, the Bible was originally written in Greek and Hebrew. At Dallas Seminary back in the 70s, you had to take three years of Greek and two years of Hebrew. Dallas Seminary is the only four-year seminary; others were three. That's because DTS emphasizes understanding biblical languages.

I majored in Old Testament (OT), so I had to take extra

Hebrew courses. One of them was called Rapid Hebrew Reading. That title kept me up at night! The fish really wanted to jump back into the water. But I chose the OT major for a reason. I liked reading the Old Testament and really wanted to understand it better. So, after meeting with a professor who guided new students and their studies, I picked Old Testament as my major.

Most of the OT students in that Rapid Hebrew Reading course were studying to be seminary professors, teaching Hebrew or OT Studies. So, it was required for them. But there I was—a former defensive back from the NFL.

The professor would put Hebrew verbs on the board, and he would ask one of us to parse the verb. Sooo embarrassing for me. I would jokingly ask for hints just to relieve some pressure. The prof couldn't help but smile. I'd hear a giggle or two from some of the students. I often felt like standing up and saying, "Any of you Hebrew nerds think you could cover Bob Hayes of the Dallas Cowboys? Huh? Do ya? HUH?"

Then there were the Greek classes. Same thing. The professor would put Greek words on the board and ask a student to parse them (I didn't know that word until seminary. "Parse" means to divide, for example, a sentence, into its different parts, and explain how the parts relate to each other). Then, he would also talk about a passage of Scripture in Greek and point out the importance of knowing the original language to have a clear meaning of the text. I loved that part.

One time, the prof was going into great detail in the Greek. He stopped and asked if there were any questions. A student named Reese Lester (good ol' country boy from Georgia) raised his hand. The professor, Dr. Zane Hodges, said, "Yes, Mr. Reese, may I help you?"

Reese then said, "Well, Dr. Hodges, I haven't understood a thing you've said for the last ten minutes." Everyone had a chuckle.

Then Professor Zane Hodges apologized laughingly and a funny look came on his face. He looked down at his student list and said, "Oh my, your last name is Lester and I have been calling you Mr. Reese."

Then without missing a beat, Mr. Reese said, "Aw, that's okay, Mr. Zane." We all had a laugh over that.

I had been wanting to meet Reese, so after class I introduced myself. I told him that he seemed to be struggling in class like me. I told him how I couldn't understand how so many of the students already knew so much about Greek. Reese said he went to see Professor Hodges and asked him the same question. He found out that many students had gone to Bible colleges and studied Greek there. Neither one of us had ever heard of a Bible college. So, that exchange with Reese made me feel a little better. Maybe the fish was learning to breathe the air. Reese became a beloved pastor and will be missed by many as he went to be with the Lord recently.

I could go into great detail on the grind of seminary, but it was also fascinating. Greek and Hebrew were very interesting at times, but my favorite courses were Church History and the Bible courses where professors would teach through the Bible (about three months on several books like Genesis through Leviticus) pretty much verse-by-verse. I really feel like a blessed man having had the opportunity to experience these in-depth biblical studies. Your faith grows and grows as you see how practical the Bible is for us down-to-earth human beings.

Our Creator wants his people to live a completely full life. God has always desired a close, personal relationship with his creation, and that becomes so clear as you look deeply into the Scripture. Especially as you see the sacrifice God's own Son was willing to go through.

And that close relationship is always there for someone who has experienced God's forgiveness. That is, to believe that God's Son, Jesus Christ, died on a cross, taking upon his perfect, sinless body God's judgment for our sins. God should have sent all people to hell because of their sinful nature, but he offered redemption, through faith in Christ, knowing that "…all have sinned and fall short of the glory of God" (Romans 3:23).

Seminary gave me a heavy dose of God's truth. God's forgiveness and grace grew more and more captivating. My faith grew more and more inspired. My peace and understanding of life grew more informed and secure. All of that to educate, support, and encourage me to some kind of full-time ministry, even though every believer who reads his Bible will experience the same.

So, there you have it. My seminary career in a nutshell.

FOOTBALL, SEMINARY STYLE

So now I was a "holy man" all involved in seminary (stop giggling). I hoped my thoughts would be pure and my words would always be encouraging. Then along came an independent seminary from California, Talbot Seminary. A darn good seminary by reputation.

Through certain people, Dallas Theological Seminary (DTS) received a challenge from Talbot to a flag football game. They would come to Dallas and play us. Hmmm. Willing to go that far and spend that kind of money for a flag football game.

Well, the sport competition gene went to work in the minds of old ex-jocks as you might say. We had some good former football players at DTS. The word got around and a meeting was held. It was a short meeting. Where do we play and when? This would be a good break from studies.

Actually, this Talbot bunch didn't give us much time. They were coming in about two weeks. And, after a little research, we found out that this team was big-time in California and won most of their games. Hmmm, again.

The day arrived and the game was on. It wasn't a sold-out crowd (our wives and a few students), but Dr. John Walvoord, president of DTS, was fired up as a former football player himself (Wheaton College, Illinois). I'm not sure what he expected. For one thing, we only had time to practice once. That was bad. But there was a bigger problem. None of us—that's right, none of us—had ever played flag football!

The moment arrived, and we ran onto the field in our

165

makeshift uniforms. We were a ragtag army: some DTS T-shirts from the seminary bookstore, normal shorts, and a few Bermudas. But we were greeted by a slick-looking ball club in nice, matching shorts and tops. *Well,* we thought, *here we go.*

We kicked off first and here they came. They moved the ball passing and running. We had some big tough "studs," but that doesn't count in flag football—speed, agility, and passing get the job done. I'll never forget this one guy, we'll call him Cowboy, who was one of our 8 starters (only 10 on the team). Seems like he was in on every play, but not in a good way.

You see, in flag ball you stop a runner by pulling one of two flags snapped to a kind of belt around his waist (ends, running backs, QB, etc.). Well, Cowboy had a hard time grabbing the flag (a learned skill), so he would simply grab the runner somewhere, anywhere, and hold him long enough to pull the flag. That became a 10-yard penalty on us every time, so Talbot players came quickly down the field, shall we say. We thought after each of about five penalties he would catch on. He didn't, and then they were on the 10 yard line, about to score on their first drive.

Next, we forgot we were representing Dallas Theological Seminary, the Harvard of seminaries as we liked to say. I mean, you'd think a seminary would be where future Christian workers, pastors, and teachers were trained. And you'd think we'd have been aware of our wives, other students, their wives, profs, and even Dr. Walvoord in the stands. But no, we were not. In fact, the song "The Heat is On" comes to mind as I try to describe what happened next.

We turned into fire-breathing, dragon-mad, righteously an-gry players. Someone told Cowboy to "stop grabbing the run-ners!" That comment did not help Cowboy's attitude. He looked at the accuser and answered, as if he were carefully translating a word from the Greek: "I'm not grabbing, I'm tack-ling! And if they come my way, I'm not going to let them spin around and dance their way into the end zone! Understand?" I guess we did. And then it happened.

Those Talbot boys were no dummies. They knew how to quickly pick up penalty yards by now. They ran to Cowboy's side and he flew into action, putting what is known in football as a form tackle on the running back—forehead to the chest—and no helmet! He then grabbed and pulled both legs forward, landing the runner on his back, and came down on him with his head still in his chest. This halfback may have been smaller, but he forgot that he was representing Talbot Seminary and he came up swinging!

Oh, what a scene. These soon-to-be preachers were swing-ing fists and knocking jaws. A few (not many!) cooler heads came to the rescue before too much bloodshed stained the sem-inary field. I can see it all like it happened yesterday. What a mess!

The next day, some of the holier-than-thou, egg-head stu-dents made sarcastic comments like, "Nice fight last night." Af-ter too much of that, I told one of them, "How about a nice fight right now?"

Well, in case you're wondering, we won the game by one point! Not much handshaking afterwards as we departed the field. I'm not sure if the moon was out and the stars were shining—I was too busy getting out of there.

Talbot never forgot that game. The next year, they called for a rematch in California with their home crowd. I'm not sure how, but Dr. Walvoord found the money to fly us all to California. And I think we only had one practice when we got there. We did have a "be nice" talk.

Talbot had a pregame dinner where both teams came together. Then, I suppose, in a teasing sort of way, one of their players from the previous year got up to say a few words— which he shouldn't have. And, before he spoke, he showed a film clip of the fight the year before. Which he shouldn't have. Whatever he said after that, it was sarcastic and smart-aleck. It did not set well.

So, we had a little team meeting. After the fun of a free ride to California and some relief from studies at seminary, we put on our game faces. We left that night ready to face them again.

The next night, just before the game, we came up with a plan for our eight-man team. Instead of rushing their QB with just the normal two down linemen and the three linebackers helping on runs and dropping back into zones on passes, with three defensive backs deeper—we made another plan.

We decided to take a chance by rushing the two down lineman and the three linebackers on every play. That put more pressure on us defensive backs, but we accepted the challenge. This year we had some speed—and more brains than brawn. And sometimes you just stumble onto an idea that works.

The QB had to rush to get plays and passes off and we

pulled his flag before he did, or it would've been a poor pass. We actually intercepted several passes in the first half of the game. I remember one of their players walking down the sideline (both teams on the same side) and telling us that we outsmarted them with our rush. Well, we won and still can say we are two and zero in DTS flag football!

That was back in 1979. Where are you, Talbot? And, really, honestly, I can say that winning those two games was as exciting as winning Super Bowl V with the Baltimore Colts back in January of 1970. Well, maybe.

HEBREW & LOADING TRUCKS

In those days, what hit me hard was not a big ol' lineman slamming into me. What hit me—even harder—was the fact that all my football money was almost gone. I had to find a job.

Not having to work for the first three years of seminary was a great blessing even though Janice worked as a substitute teacher in the public schools and at the Market Center in Dallas.

I ended up with a job on the loading docks of a big trucking company. That was not exciting. But I have to confess, it was very humbling. There I was, with some tough old men, loading freight. They didn't know me, or even care to know me. They just wanted me to get those trucks loaded.

I worked from 4 p.m. to 12 p.m. on several nights. Mostly it was daytime work; they helped me arrange my schedule around classes since the owner of the company was a Dallas

Seminary donor. I'd been through grinders before, so thank you Coach Stallings. It definitely was not fun and between Hebrew and truck loading—I had to find another job!

Wait a minute, I thought. I had worked for Texas A&M in development. And Dallas Seminary is a private seminary. They must do some fundraising to stay alive. So, I made an appointment to meet a Mr. George Rutenbar.

I didn't realize 'til we met that he had played professional baseball. We hit it off right away, each of us exchanging funny stories. He looked at me and said, "Tommy, with your background, you are exactly what we have been looking for. Can you start work right away? How many hours are you taking this semester?" I filled him in and said I could start tomorrow. I have never been so excited about a job in all my life. I got to work for a wonderful man, graduate of DTS, pro baseball player, and great preacher and Bible teacher. I couldn't wait to tell Janice!

A PERFECT JOB

Development work was a perfect job for future ministry. I traveled around Dallas and visited donors or potential donors. I met the finest Christian people in the world and most of them clearly saw the value of Dallas Theological Seminary. Their financial support would train future leaders in the Christian faith. And, as a student, I could share firsthand the excellent training and professors I had.

Most of the professors also taught Sunday school classes in churches around the Dallas area. So, those folks I visited would light up when I talked about their Sunday school teachers from a student perspective. It was a fun job and seemed to fit better with my Greek and Hebrew than loading trucks! It lightened up my load, that's for sure. Although, writing this now, I can see what God was doing by putting me on the loading docks. Those dock loaders are as important to him as any pro athlete.

LOOKING FOR A PASTOR

The big day arrived. Graduation. May 1983. I crossed the stage and received my diploma for a ThM (Master of Theology) degree. Took me five years (four-year curriculum) to get it since I worked for DTS while a student. I didn't cross a stage at A&M after graduating because I was over in Italy visiting my older sister and her husband in the Navy. So, this experience was new and unforgettable.

But now what to do? What was next for Not So Fast? I'd been thinking about it, wondering, and then the phone rang. It was Ted Koy. He and his wife, Lynn, were friends from Bryan, where he graduated from the Texas A&M veterinary school.

Ted had also been a fullback for the University of Texas and played six years in the NFL. A little story here: When we met for the first time, I told him I was still mad at him. He got that "What?" look (I get that a lot) as I told him what I tell all former fullbacks. I say, "Why don't you guys try to sidestep us little defensive backs so we can tackle you from the side? But noooo, you fullbacks take great pleasure in just running over us poor little defensive backs. What can we do? We try to grab a foot, and then you drag us 10 painful yards, stepping all over us. And worse, while everyone's jumping on us, guess who's at the bottom of that pileup, 800 pounds of linemen heaped on top of us? Me!"

Back to the story. Sorry, I had to get my frustration with fullbacks off my chest—no pun intended. Ted had heard about me graduating from seminary, and he now had a vet clinic in Georgetown, Texas. He was attending a church that was look- ing for a pastor and called to see if I was interested.

I really had to think about that—since the only reason I went to seminary was to understand the Bible better. But I needed a job, which is not the best reason to be a pastor. Ted wanted to know if I was interested. I wasn't sure if I was inter- ested, or not interested. Just wasn't sure what to think, or do.

So, Janice and I prayed and decided to visit Georgetown and check it out.

CHAPTER 13
MAXWELL IN GEORGETOWN

PASTOR TOMMY

In Georgetown, Janice and I sat down with the elders of Grace Bible Church. The former pastor had also graduated from Dallas Seminary, but decided pastoring was not his calling and went to law school and became an attorney. Well, they interviewed me and about a week later, called and offered me the position. I really believe they wanted Janice more than me. The only positions I had been used to were football positions. This was different. A big kind of different.

We decided to accept their invitation. And so, in August of 1983, we moved to Georgetown, with all that a move entails, and we settled into a new life and, for me, a new role.

I would be preaching/teaching the Bible to a group of people who had come to church to hear what I had to say. And, this was a weekly deal. However, I liked the idea of encouraging folks in the faith. On the other hand, I've never felt comfortable as a public speaker, but, once I'm up there, and get going, I relax.

Truth is, I'm most comfortable sitting at a table with men around me, teaching the Bible—and having fun with it. I had that opportunity while in seminary with a group of businessmen who met at Jack Turpin's tennis facility in Dallas. I learned a lot just watching how Jack would interact with fellow businessmen. I have to smile because it seems the Lord always puts me with a group of real characters. Very distinct personalities. I have come to realize that I am somewhat of a different character myself (ask Janice), so we all get along just fine.

I never thought I'd be asked to lead a church, but there I was, former pro football player, truck loader, Hebrew student, insurance salesman, and now a pastor.

It was exciting to see that what I'd learned I could put into practice, teaching and encouraging others. Training had become opportunity. "Go therefore and make disciples of all nations…" (Matthew 28:19).

Those three years pastoring right after seminary were very interesting and rewarding years. The church really grew, and we made some wonderful friends. However, it came to an end rather unexpectedly. There's not much to tell about this. There was a meeting, there were conversations to discuss the future of the church…and it became clear that the elders' vision and goals for the church did not align with my goals, gifts, and vision for the church. We parted friends, but it was a difficult transition, to put it lightly. Still, as Scripture encourages us to do in difficulties, we trust the God who holds our times in his hand (Psalm 31:15).

Well, really it was just another NSF moment, like the original one, when I stepped into a position and then Coach Madden moved me out of it. My Lord, my Master, my Coach (capital C) would, once again, point my crazy life in a new direction.

Our sovereign God (there's that theological word again) would use my time as a pastor to groom me for the next stage of his calling. Leaving the church, in what seemed to be a down moment in my life, was really the start of the best part of my life.

In fact, being a pastor prepared me to talk to other pastors about Coaches Outreach, and to be careful when talking to church members interested in joining us. When we interview a potential lay leader, we ask about his church. If he's already involved, we don't want to put more responsibility on his shoulders. If we find someone who qualifies and really has a heart for our ministry, we visit his pastor to bring him into the process.

We also invite a person and/or a pastor to look over our doctrinal statement, and clearly explain that, as a para-church organization, we're not interested in draining churches by taking away key leadership that is so important to church life and effectiveness.

When the process continues, we go into more detail, explaining how our material makes it easy to facilitate a study. A leader can prep in one hour and lead a study in one hour, and still have a very dynamic ministry time. That insight and church-friendly process was the direct result of my pastoral experience.

But back to when the down moment felt like a down moment.

Once again, Maxwell needed a job. Now, in Georgetown, where would he find it? These were tough days, and I found myself sinking to the bottom, struggling to look up.

During that time, someone told me that reading through the Psalms helped them conquer their depression. I dove into the Psalms and seriously—it saved my life. God became more real than I could have ever imagined. My time at seminary paled in comparison.

I COULDN'T DO IT RIGHT

Several months later, now in 1986, desperate for work, I interviewed with a manager at our life insurance company and, in turn, got a job selling life insurance, making appointments over the phone. Hadn't done that before. And probably for good reason.

Sitting in a typical insurance sales meeting was humbling to say the least. I felt like I was back in Hebrew class. The district manager would look around the room, asking about how many people you called the week before. Uh-oh.

Some guys had called 25, some 50, some 100. I sat in an office right next to a fella who was always calling people—all day long! If you're reading this, and you do this for a living, my hat goes off to you. Good job! But I couldn't do it. Couldn't do it right, anyway.

One problem was, I enjoyed talking to people instead of

moving toward a possible sale. These conversations were always long and in-depth, many times enjoyable. But that was bad according to my manager. I felt like a lost puppy again, as he scolded me.

"Tommy, call to make an appointment, not to chitchat about their pets. You're averaging five calls a day. You'll starve to death doing that! What are you doing, man?" Well, I did sell a few policies, but if Janice had not been working, we probably would have been starving to death.

INTO THE A&M HALL OF FAME

I guess the ol' telephone has played a big part in my life. And, like the call from Madden, a few of those calls turned out to be life-changers.

I was sitting in my office in downtown Georgetown when I got a call from a representative of the Texas A&M athletic department. A smile came to my face as the caller congratulated me on entering the A&M Sports Hall of Fame. That honor had never crossed my mind and I couldn't quite believe it was happening. A surprised, very blessed kind of emotion came over me. I remember it very clearly.

I must have called Janice after hearing the happy news, since she was always my first call. The local paper, the Williamson County Sun, printed an article titled, "AGGIE ACHIEVER: Double Duty Earns Tommy Maxwell Texas A&M Hall of Fame Honors." Janice still has the article clipped out and tucked away. I remember telling the reporter—and they printed it—that I almost fell out of my chair when I got the news. That pretty well captured the feeling of the moment!

The article covered A&M's victory over Alabama in the 1968 Cotton Bowl. Let me recap: This was a big upset since Alabama was picked to beat Texas A&M by 20 points! I intercepted a pass that set up our first touchdown and later caught a touchdown pass to put us ahead of Alabama.

Since we're talking about it, that play even got mentioned in *Bebes and the Bear*, published in 2019. The paragraph said, "Aggie safety Tommy Maxwell responded on Alabama's next possession. Maxwell—A&M's two-way marvel—intercepted a Stabler pass and returned it to A&M's 18 yard line." Never thought of myself as a "marvel," but that's quite a compliment.

Among other things, the Sun Sports editor described me as anchoring the Colts defense, holding the Dallas Cowboys to 13 points in Super Bowl V. I didn't start in that Super Bowl because of an earlier injury, but I was on most of the special teams. Jimmy Duncan had taken my place and he did a great job.

But it wasn't until the A&M Hall of Fame banquet for that year, 1991, which was a formal evening, that I fully realized how thankful I was to have that honor. My mom and dad were there along with Janice and our daughters, Lezley and Lauren. Makes me smile with that warm feeling again, just thinking about it now.

ANOTHER CALL, ANOTHER TOMMY

As time went on, slowly but surely, the wind was dying and my sails were just hanging there, lifeless.

On my day off, I sat in my home office and wondered if that wind would ever pick up again. The Psalms always lifted my spirit, but like the psalmist, I asked, "Why are you cast down, O my soul..." (Psalm 42:5).

Then the silence was broken by—you guessed it—another phone call.

The year was 1998. The voice was Tommy Cox, a coach I knew in Austin, Texas. I'd spoken to his football team a couple of times. Excitedly he said, "Tommy, I sent a letter out to all the coaches in Austin to gauge their interest in starting a Bible study. I've already received calls or notes from 10 of them who want to come."

I said, "Tommy, that's super!"

"And I have some good news for you," he continued. "You're teaching it!"

I heard him laugh, but I heard another voice in my heart saying, "Tommy, I'm not through with you yet."

That Bible study came together about two weeks later and there were 15 coaches there, looking at me, ready to go. Eddie Joseph, director of the Coaches Association of Austin, made sure we had coffee and donuts. That's important for those early morning Bible studies!

What a great group. We took turns reading through Bible passages and discussed the details, verse-by-verse. More and

179

more I began to see how relevant it was to their lives.

The Scripture was really coming alive to them. As weeks went on, they shared how much they enjoyed the time together. They were learning, but also making friends with opponents from other schools they competed against. That got my attention. For the first time, I began to understand the heart of great Christian coaches. I couldn't wait to get there—bright and early—every Thursday morning at 6:45 a.m.

When we were finishing up for the spring semester, I asked them if they wanted to have some kind of get together with their wives. They were all in. Then the thought came to me. Jack Turpin, in Dallas, owned T Bar M, that beautiful retreat center in New Braunfels, Texas.

The next week, I asked the coaches if they'd be interested in having something like a marriage retreat, there at T Bar M, after the spring semester. They were all for that, too!

So, I called Jack and told him about our new Bible study and the coaches' desire to get together. I asked him how much it would be to rent T Bar M for about 15 couples. Jack then hit me with this. "Tommy, I had a coach in high school who was like a dad to me. He changed my life. You get those coaches to T Bar M and don't worry about the cost."

I was floored at Jack's generosity, his heart for coaches. But at the same time, I've always believed that dollars show commitment, so I charged them $25 ($800 value) that first year. And guess what? We had 17 coaching couples at that first retreat and now, we have had over 100 retreats, each averaging 50 couples, in five different states, since that first one in 1993!

Today, these retreats cost our ministry, Coaches Outreach, over $30,000 each summer because we pay about three-fourths of the cost for each couple who comes. Marriages are always strengthened and many have come to Christ during the conferences. Coaching couples deserve first class marriage conferences and we provide that, I'm proud and grateful, to say.

We were not that organized that first year, and the couples just went with the flow. We decided to pick some older Christian couples and have a sort of a question-and-answer period between coaching husbands (four selected men faced all the wives) and wives (four selected wives answered questions from all the men).

In a separate meeting area, the four ladies would answer questions that the men asked. At the same time, in their own meeting area, the four men would answer questions that the ladies asked. Brilliant idea, right? (Think loud, irritating game buzzer sound). Not So Fast strikes again.

The whole thing flopped. Well, to be clear, the ladies got it right. The coach's wives were articulate, wise, and insightful about their roles. The men just sat there, listened, and never spoke! The four men coaches "fumbled the ball" as the wives hit the coaches with tough questions. It was painful to hear the guys search for different ways to say, "I don't know."

I remember checking on how it was going. I left the wives meeting all excited. However, on the way to the other group, one of the wives stopped me, a panicked look on her face. "Oh, Tommy," she blurted out. "It's a disaster! The wives are all over the poor coaches. The men are sitting there, tongue-tied. Some of us older wives are defending the coaches—but what should we do?" Like one of the men coaches, I didn't have an answer!

We decided to let it blow over, lesson learned. Before the weekend came to an end, everyone actually laughed about the Q&A disaster. And it became obvious to the four coaches and four wives leading, the easy-to-see difference between men and women. The men were oblivious to how the home was run and what the kids were feeling, but the wives had the pulse of every little turn and tension in the home. We learned a lot of lessons from that retreat and the many that followed.

BLAST FROM THE PAST

About this time in our journey, I was attending an Aggie Club BBQ in Austin. This was twenty years after losing that game to SMU and their amazing QB, Mr. Ines Perez.

I walked in and some guys motioned me to come over. They said, "Guess who that little guy is over there?"

I had no clue till one of them said, "That's Ines Perez." I couldn't believe it.

What was he doing at an Aggie function? I went over to introduce myself and ask why he was there. I faced him, puttin' on the anger. "I'm still mad about that game on national TV where you fired off a bunch of passes and beat us!" Then, smiling, I said, "I was in that game!"

He looked up at me with a half-grin and said he was sorry. He explained that he had a good friend who was an Aggie who had invited him and then he said, "I love Aggies. I'm more well-known by Aggies for that one game than I am from my four years at SMU."

It turned out that Ines was a well-respected head coach at Round Rock High School (near Georgetown) where he had picked up the nickname, "The Little General." Great nickname.

He told me that he had just received a letter from Coach Tommy Cox in Austin about a Bible study at the Texas HS Coaches Association offices. That was amazing! (No coincidences).

I told him that Coach Cox had asked me to lead that study. Ines ended up coming to it and loved the interaction with other coaches. The dynamic of this Bible study was very special. These men competed against one another on a weekly basis, but as we studied the Bible together, they each began to grow spiritually and relationally in their callings as coaches.

After a few weeks of study, Ines spoke up and said, "I took some boys to an FCA conference, and I received Jesus as my Savior."

That was exciting! I had to know more. "Tell us about that, Ines."

"It was very special. I'd never done that before—put my faith in Jesus Christ as my personal Savior. Christ isn't just someone who saves others. He's someone who has saved me! And I don't just hope I'll go to heaven; he promises me I will go to heaven."

It was from this Bible study, with other coaches talking

183

about God and their personal relationship, that Ines felt comfortable enough to share his newfound faith. And be himself.

Ines had a good sense of humor. I always asked one of the coaches to pray after the study. I would make sure they were comfortable with that before I asked them. I asked Ines if he would be comfortable saying a prayer. He said, "I guess so."

Well, the next week I asked Ines to close in prayer and he said this. "I will pray, but I cannot pray for Coach Cox" (who was there that morning).

A few coaches smiled and I asked Ines why he couldn't pray for Coach Cox. Ines said, "I am playing Coach Cox's team this Friday and I do not want God to bless him." We all cracked up, including Coach Cox.

God was sure working all those years ago in that first college game versus SMU. That loss to SMU, on national TV, pointed me to Ines. And God had ordained Ines to be in that coaches' study. Can God do that? Yes, indeed. Makes life fascinating, and provides an underlying sense of security, knowing a sovereign God is in complete control of his creation.

All the coaches in that first study in Austin were great coaches. And, they were the start of Coaches Outreach. Ines went on to be the athletic director for Lubbock, Texas. Eddie Joseph continued to make sure our meetings always had coffee and donuts. In fact, to this day, they still meet together every Tuesday morning.

Things got going. In June 1992, after going through the application process, the Coaches Outreach 501c3 status was official. I wasn't full-time yet, but the ministry was coming together. But I had no idea about the great things God had in store.

ANOTHER MOVE?

On the heels of the experiences of the early coaches Bible studies, and the first marriage retreat, and with the placement of radio pastor and author Chuck Swindoll as the new president of Dallas Theological Seminary, a new NSF assignment headed my way.

The year was 1993. This time it wasn't a phone call. The DTS director of development and his assistant drove from Dallas to Georgetown to meet with me. We sat down, and in so many words, they invited me to move back to Dallas and once again work in development (fundraising) for the seminary.

I talked to Janice. Well, more accurately, Janice had a talk with me! I guess I was pretty insensitive to her feelings when I told her about moving back to Dallas. I kind of dumped it on her, acting like it should happen, just like that.

I didn't realize just how many times we had moved—like 9 times in 10 years of marriage. That was way too many nests my sweet Twirly Bird had to build. I could tell you how it went but, as I did in telling our dating story, I'd better let Janice tell you, in her words, how that decision played out...

DALLAS BOUND

From Janice Maxwell

I remember it very clearly. Early in May, Lauren had graduated from high school, and Tommy said, "I think they're going to ask us to move back to Dallas so I can work at DTS again, as part of a team. So, we'll need to know what to tell them."

I snapped back. "That's easy! Tell 'em no."

Tommy came back with, "Janice, it's my job."

The fact was, I did not want to move back to Dallas. But Chuck Swindoll had just become president of the seminary, and they wanted Tommy's help. But I just didn't want to budge. I knew the Lord wasn't pleased with me, and I didn't care. I was definitely not in the Lord's will, with my stubborn (okay, defiant) attitude. I remember Tommy saying, "Well, let's just pray about it."

In June, I apologized. Yes, over a month later. I told Tommy I wanted us to do what the Lord wanted, so if that meant moving back to Dallas, I was all in. I said we'd have to sell our house, and with two daughters in college, I might need to get a job there, or I stay behind and keep working until I find something there.

Soon after, I was at a speech pathology conference in San Antonio. Tommy called and said, "Well, I've made up my mind on what we're going to do."

"Okay, what's your decision?"

"We're going back to Dallas."

This time, I was ready for it. "Okay," I said calmly. "Alright.

That's what we'll do." We talked and hung up. And I burst into tears!

Back from the conference, Tommy and I began freshening up the house. We put extra furniture in a friend's garage and had an open house, Saturday and Sunday. A couple came—that weekend—and said they definitely wanted to buy our home. Wow. Two weeks later I was offered a job in Coppell, not far from Dallas. We sold the house, and another blessing came to us: friends in the DFW metroplex needed someone to watch their home while they were away for quite a while. We moved right in. God is so good.

Looking back, the only good thing about all those moves was that both Tommy and I could relate to all the moves that coaches and their wives had to make. We could truly empathize, and we never found a couple who had moved as much as we did. So, the coaches and couples that we would sometimes counsel could always see that if we were "still alive and kickin'," they could make it, too.

CHAPTER 14
COACHES OUTREACH
BEGINS

TOMMY & CHUCK

In September 1993, we found ourselves back in Dallas, Texas.

We rented a small house which, though it worked fine for us, was a difficult adjustment for the girls. New schools, new friends, and really, a whole new environment, came at a stage in life when you want things around you to stay the same. It had to be tough on them.

But, like their mom, they were troopers. I never remember them complaining. I'm sure Janice had some talks with them about Dad's "calling," which took a while for me to figure out, considering how I bounced from place to place and job to job.

We have been blessed by being dependent on the Lord. You can see from reading the Scripture that biblical characters made a lot of "faith moves." All the moves going one way and then another in my life (NSF) gave me a tested, but solid, dependence on God's grace and guidance. And, I guess, a crazy title for this little book!

Maybe it will land in the hands of another couple working their way along life's path, with kids, and big moves they are questioning. Maybe like a missionary family, or a military family. Or a coaching family!

Our walk along life's path has brought me to an "active dependence" on the Lord. I'll explain that a little bit later.

Going back to work for Dallas Seminary was like taking a breath of fresh air. And the head guy was Chuck Swindoll! And get this. There were times, as part of my job, I would go pick him up at the airport. I felt like I was picking up a Hollywood star! People would point at him and some would actually want his autograph.

Chuck had a magic way with people. Anyone who spent two minutes with Chuck walked away feeling like his best friend. He would engage people with great questions, and they would share their lives with him. I loved watching that.

At a DTS retreat in the summer of 1994, our development staff was having lunch together at a local restaurant. Chuck was with us. A young male waiter walked up to the table and asked, "Excuse me, are you Chuck Swindoll?" Right away, Chuck zeroed in on this young man, asking him questions, getting to know him. The waiter said he was a new believer and listened to Chuck every day driving to work. Chuck just smiled and we all started leaving while the young man cleared away our dishes.

We returned to the bus and after we all loaded, we started

looking for Chuck (he would rather be called Chuck than Dr. Swindoll or Pastor). Someone got off the bus to look for him. Turned out, Chuck slipped away to find the owner of the restaurant and asked if he could have a few minutes with this young waiter.

I can guarantee you this: that young man will never be the same, and I would love to have heard that conversation—and take a peek at that young man's life today. Chuck is a gifted preacher because he loves people like his Savior does.

While working for Dallas Seminary, I could go sit in on classes and listen to professors give great lectures on the Bible. I also went to campus chapel services where I heard some of the best authors and speakers in the country. And then, of course, since it was my job, I made trips to visit donors, sometimes taking me around the country.

I traveled all over the place, from "Nowhere, Ohio" to big cities, or small, busy towns. I would find the house, meet the donor, and make new friends. I didn't even have to sell them an insurance policy!

But as we spoke, and as I flashed my Super Bowl V ring, I realized that football fans were everywhere, and they loved hearing football stories. We would talk about their lives, their families, and of course how much DTS appreciated their support. My work for Dallas Seminary never felt like work for me. I just asked questions, cared, and listened. It was almost like pastoring, wasn't it?

191

REACHING OUT TO COACHES

Yet another move! This time, 1994, to Grapevine, Texas, while I was still working for Dallas Seminary. The girls were both at Texas Tech University. Texas Aggie friends, please forgive me. It turned out to be a great experience for both of them.

By this time, I knew these coaches Bible studies were having a profound effect and were well-attended. I saw the value as biblical truth played out in coaches' lives and coaching couples' lives through the marriage retreats, though I didn't quite know how to grow the ministry.

As I mentioned, I'd visited with an attorney to start a 501c3 to allow this ministry to have a non-profit status. That way, people could receive a tax deduction for supporting the work. So support could grow. So the ministry could grow. And there was a location established.

My main work was visiting DTS donors around Texas and other states. On occasion, I'd stop by schools at lunch time to share the ministry of Coaches Outreach. The more I met with high school coaches, the more my respect grew for these dedicated men and women.

I would travel out to coaches in Dallas, all over Texas, and other states. That was relatively easy.

It was not easy to make appointments with high school coaches. They don't work that way. The best thing to do, I found out, was to just go to the school and find the coach's office. And if he or she wasn't there, I usually went out to the gym, or the field. They were usually out there—somewhere.

After a while, I developed a good feel for where they would be. I'd walk up and knock on the door of the head coach. "Hello? Coach. Do you have five minutes?" On a good day, I would hear, "Yeah, come in."

I would give a brief introduction and ask if they had ever heard of Coaches Outreach. Sometimes I would have received their name from another coach and that made it a lot easier to ask for their time and attention. Sometimes it was a cold call, emphasis on the "cold." Coaches could be skeptical, uninterested, or just flat out too busy.

But coaches are curious people (looking for that winning edge), so they were often curious why I came to see them, or why another coach would've sent me.

MY SPIEL

Many times, especially with head coaches, things would grind to a halt after I explained my purpose. They wrapped it up before I could start into it, saying they didn't have time for a Bible study—and neither did their coaches. There was no room in the schedule.

My answer to that was this: "Well, coach, time is a very special thing for you and your coaches. However, if just one coach would want a Bible study, we would find an outstanding person from the community to facilitate it. He would be loyal to you, and the one coach. We would require this person to visit with you, and if for any reason you didn't like this person, we'd take the hit and find somebody else. And if that didn't work, I'd come out and facilitate the study myself." That would often turn things around, and after months of the one-coach Bible study, more and more coaches would show up.

But when the coach was open to hearing it, I'd give my "spiel." It usually started with a short history of Coaches Outreach.

While talking, I'd slide the Super Bowl ring on my finger. I had...technique. I would always try to pick a position that showed off the ring. Maybe scratch my chin or rub my eye, ring finger in prominent view. I joke with people that I would even pick my nose with my ring finger. The coaches would always see it and ask about it. Sometimes, many times, they already knew what the ring was for. I believe the Lord had it in his plan to use that ring to make sure his truth got to coaches.

Then I would present four reasons why coaches really liked our Bible study material.

1. You will learn more about the Bible than you could ever imagine.

2. Your coaches will grow closer together.

3. Your involvement in our studies will make you a better coach.

4. You will have more peace than you've ever experienced during your sports season.

They always smiled at the last one since there is no job that brings as much stress as coaching. I would show them how our studies were fascinating and down-to-earth, and what a lesson looked like.

Also, I guaranteed that by doing four short 20-minute lessons a week, along with an hour a week in a meeting with other coaches, they would know more about a book in the Bible than anyone in their church. Since all coaches are very competitive, they liked that last part best.

Starting up Bible studies was my favorite thing to do at Coaches Outreach. The studies were multiplying, and I couldn't have been happier. Especially rewarding was the moment when a coach would send a note or call sharing how much they were learning and how much they enjoyed the interaction with other coaches from their school or other schools.

QUIT YOUR DAY JOB, TOMMY

Another great moment happened in 1996, at the close of a marriage retreat, when a good friend, Coach Donnie Snodgrass, handed me a three-page letter, handwritten on legal-sized paper.

Here was a detailed, heartfelt outline explaining why Coaches Outreach should be—seriously needed to be—a full-time ministry. Donnie felt it was ready to go, given the structure of Bible studies and marriage retreats, and he felt it was time I "quit my day job," as they say, to go full-time with the ministry.

I knew he put a lot of time and thought into it. It was the perfect game plan for the ministry and spoke right to me, since

I was not a coach and really needed to hear and read what a coach thought.

Janice was driving us home, so I called my friend, Ray Biles, who, at that time, was the head football coach at the high school where Donnie also coached. I told Ray about Donnie's three-page letter and asked if Janice and I could come see him and Julie.

Ray pretty much gave me the same advice Donnie wrote in the letter. God sovereignly directed these two coaches who both challenged me and had me running some 100s just like Coach Taylor at A&M.

The takeaway is this: coaches started Coaches Outreach and they "coached me up" (challenged me) to realize I could be doing a lot more to help coaches than I thought I could.

THE FOG CLEARS

Spring 1997. Things were really rolling now. We still lived in Grapevine, with me still working for Dallas Seminary, still having our summer marriage retreats and starting up CO Bible studies. Enter the game: Mr. Norm Miller and his company, Interstate Batteries.

I'd enjoyed visiting with Norm on a recent trip to Israel with the seminary. So, on one of my meet-the-donors rounds, I just dropped in on him to say hello. Sitting in his office, there was small talk, and Norm asked, out of the blue, "Tell me about that coaching ministry you started."

Funny thing, I found out later that Jack Turpin had mentioned it to Norm. Well, I perked up and started telling him all about it. He was enjoying the stories, laughing, and that always keeps me going. After my hyped-up monologue, Norm turned serious. He gave me a businesslike look and said, "Tommy, you work for Dallas Seminary, but your heart is in Coaches Outreach."

I melted in my chair. I'd been in a fog for a long time and suddenly it cleared away. I've not shared this with anyone except Janice, but here it is. I'd been wrestling with where my heart was—but always dismissed it. Here's why.

I'd been thinking, praying, really stressing about going full-time with Coaches Outreach, but I had to keep working because our funds were very low, keeping the girls in college. And, though it was tempting, I was not going to ask seminary donors about supporting Coaches Outreach while working for Dallas Seminary.

Back to the Interstate Batteries office. I was stunned by Mr. Miller's comment. I couldn't speak. I just looked at him. And he looked at me. Well, really, he looked past my face and right into my soul.

I gave in. I told Norm about my struggle. And, like a true businessman, he got right down to the finances. He asked me how much I needed a month to make it. I fumbled around with some numbers. He pulled out his checkbook and wrote a check. He handed it to me, and explained, "Tommy, you can use this to help coaches attend your next conference or you can use it as a monthly salary so you can spend all your time with Coaches

Outreach."

I'll never forget that moment. But there were more moments on the way.

Soon afterward, I had lunch with a buddy from seminary, Andy Wileman, or Andrew Wild Man as I call him. Andy pastored Grace Bible Church in Dallas. He knew about my involvement with coaches and the Bible studies and he told me—a year before I would meet with Norm—to "get after those coaches. Quit screwing around!"

He was short and stocky and talked more like a coach than a pastor. At that lunch, Andy told me about his "dysfunctional Bible study group" and one of the men in the group, All-Pro lineman John Niland of the Dallas Cowboys. Andy challenged me to go talk to John. He said he had already told John about me and Coaches Outreach.

I was a little nervous for some reason, but John and I had a great visit. He asked me what my biggest concern was about starting Coaches Outreach. Still getting used to opening up about stuff like this, I hesitated, then told him it was making my house payments. Without missing a beat, he offered to cover any house payment I couldn't make. Again, the Lord worked through one of his boys (Cowboys), to keep me going forward with Coaches Outreach. My faith was really growing.

During that year, 1997, I did it. I left Dallas Theological Seminary and went full-time with Coaches Outreach. Scan this QR code for Tommy's sports videos and interviews.

In the big picture of things, the Lord worked through several of his boys in the formation of Coaches Outreach. My good friend, Scott Henderson, and our mutual friend, Tommy Nelson, pastor of Denton Bible Church, were two of those boys, and a big part of the early formation of the ministry. I'll pass the ball to Scott here, and let him tell you a few of his stories, this one going back to 1998, in Denton, Texas.

GOSPEL BLIMPS
From Scott Henderson

During one Sunday evening service, Pastor Tommy Nelson took spiritual measurements of the members of Denton Bible Church, calling us "gospel blimps" if we attended DBC for a year and did not exercise our faith. The impact was so great on me that I can quote Pastor Nelson, "If you have been attending Denton Bible Church for over a year and you just sit there soaking up the gospel, biblical truths, etc., and not exercising your faith, you are a gospel blimp!" (Gospel blimp is a term that describes a person who floats along, keeping their distance, enjoying the ride but not really engaging with people or purpose).

Although there were probably over a thousand people at the service, I felt the Holy Spirit had singled me out. So, I invited Tommy Nelson to a chicken fried steak lunch to discuss it. Across the table, I confessed that I was worse than a gospel blimp (attending DBC for over two years as tapes and CDs accumulated), and Pastor Tommy said that he would prayerfully consider a ministry for me.

Two weeks later, Tommy called and wanted to introduce me to a guy named Tommy Maxwell, founder of a ministry called Coaches Outreach (note the timing: Tommy Maxwell had reached out to Tommy Nelson to discuss his vision for the ministry...probably stressing that he needed Lay Leaders outside the coaching profession to facilitate the Bible studies). As they say, you can't make this stuff up. God was at work, in the small details—and the large scope of building his kingdom.

I met with Tommy Maxwell and I was impressed. At this introductory meeting, he gave an overview of the vision he had for the ministry. Then, we met again. The second and third meetings were strictly to verify my fundamental beliefs. Soon after, Tommy invited me to be a Lay Leader in the north Texas regions of Denton County...I accepted. I have affectionately identified the training for the Lay Leader as the "Junction Boy's Bible Boot Camp," playing off Tommy Maxwell's A&M roots.

Starting with one, then growing to two or three of us, we would meet at Tommy's home in Grapevine, Texas for a day of one-on-one, biblically based "linebacker" drills designed to meet the spiritual objectives of ministering to coaches. By the way, these were some of the greatest moments in establishing my own personal foundation, training me to be prepared for the CO Bible studies.

At this particular time, about 15 coaches from several high

schools in the Denton area expressed interest in a Coaches Outreach Bible study. We had one Lay Leader (the first one, me), and I believe, at the first meeting, we had coaches from six area schools. We gathered together at the Radisson Hotel.

This is when the ministry stumbled onto a problem. It's not uncommon for coaches to move every year, and we found that coaches would move to a new location and want a Coaches Outreach Bible study at their new school.

This began to happen at an exponentially high rate. Quickly, the need for Lay Leaders outpaced the ministry's ability to train them. A good thing, but a pressing need. And, as is also common, it led to a breakthrough.

Coaches Outreach would need to establish a regional recruitment and training program to meet the lay leader needs for all these coaches. God met that need, raising up Lay Leaders to fulfill the expansion of the Bible studies, today many hundreds of them across multiple states.

As the ministry expanded, a phenomenon took place…God raised up retired coaches, from across various regions of the state of Texas, to volunteer in promoting the Coaches Outreach Bible studies to area high schools. Another breakthrough.

And because these coaches were very well-known, respected, and recognized within the community, the Bible studies grew even more.

Presently at Coaches Outreach, recognizing God's hand in this area, the ministry has established Field Reps as contractual positions with individuals who love the Lord and this ministry.

The results of the field rep program have successfully advanced the gospel and Bible studies to regions within a growing number of states throughout the country.

I appreciate Tommy Maxwell letting me have a place here to share this "Jazzercise history" of Coaches Outreach, from my point of view. Along with fellow board members Dan Mitchell, Tommy Teague, Jack Simmons, and more, we join to celebrate the outstanding work God has engineered in the formation of this ministry. And of course, Pastor Tommy Nelson's earliest endorsements and continuing support over the years have been a highlight of God's hand in the outward and upward growth of this ministry.

Back to me, Tommy Maxwell. I guess I just realized—we've got a lot of Tommy's involved here! Me, Tommy Cox, Tommy Nelson, and Tommy Teague. Well, it's a good name, isn't it? Anyway, my friend Tommy Cox could tell you lots of stories from the growing years of Coaches Outreach. Tommy (Cox) calls this his "Fork in the Road" story. Take it, Tommy.

FORK IN THE ROAD
From of Tommy Cox

We lost a game we should have won. Blaming the kids for the loss, I lit into them on the bus ride home. But when I saw the hurt in their eyes, I knew right away—I was wrong. I tossed and turned all night recalling what I'd said and how I'd said it. I was devastated. I called them together before practice the next day and told them how ashamed I was for my actions. And, humbled, I asked for their forgiveness.

That was a game changer for me. A proverbial "fork in the road."

I realized how selfish and destructive my coaching style was and how it affected my players both in their performance and in their lives. I knew why God called me to coach, but I was not getting it done. I prayed countless times for his power to remain faithful to what He called me to do.

I started accepting more responsibility when we had bad practices and when we played poorly on Friday night. I knew I needed to prepare better, teach more thoroughly, encourage and motivate with enthusiasm, make it fun, and most important—love them—win or lose.

This event had a major impact on my relationship with kids, really, for the rest of my entire coaching career. It taught me the importance of forming lasting friendships with them. Friendships that would continue long after their playing days.

But it made a difference in the players' performance, too. Get this: we won our last three games and qualified for the state playoffs.

Like all coaches, I love to win, and I believe God wants us to excel wherever he calls us. But I don't think he's that concerned about how many games we win. Or lose. He gave us this platform so we could love kids and lead them to Jesus for his

203

glory, not ours. To that end, I hope to hear him say to me one day, "Well done, my good and faithful servant."

CHAPTER 15

MORE COACHES, MORE OUTREACH

THE SIGN ON THE BUILDING

A while back, someone asked me, "Tommy (Maxwell), how did you start Coaches Outreach?" I answered that real quick: "I didn't. God did." I couldn't have imagined what God had in store, but he knew all along and had it prepared beforehand. I was walking along, doing the good work of trying to start coaches Bible studies. I knew the numbers of these Bible studies were growing, and I knew more and more coaches were attending, but I had no idea that, in the years to come, God would build a nationwide ministry.

So, let me get back to the story of Coaches Outreach, picking it up in 1998.

Not yet full-time with the ministry (though I was committed to that goal), I worked out of my home and began the search for an "official" office. We needed a place in Dallas, basically with a room and a phone.

My friend, Joe Furstenberg, kindly met that need. He provided an office (with a phone) at his construction business in Dallas. He even allowed us to put up a CO sign on the exterior of his building. Somehow, the sign on the building stamped Coaches Outreach as a real place. Janice and I stood there, looking at it, very grateful. I was, of course, excited!

We brought on Robert Irion and Mark Wyatt to help with organizing the addition of more Bible studies. I spent at least four days a week just meeting coaches in Texas, traveling farther east, talking about the studies as far as North Carolina. I remember taking a trip through Ohio and Idaho. I saw Amish families riding down the road in horse-drawn wagons with cars passing by. Although they chose a simplified life, I'd heard they engaged in all kinds of sports. I would have spread the ministry to them, as well, but didn't meet any Amish coaches.

To this day, I love meeting and interacting with coaches involved at all levels of sports. My mother once told me I should have chosen coaching over playing, and I don't know, maybe she was right. Then again, although players take a lot of hard knocks, coaches live in the real battle of the sports world. Especially high school coaches.

I remember a significant conversation with Coach Ken Hatfield, who played for Arkansas and was later head coach for Rice University in Houston. I gave Ken a call and he invited me to come on by.

As I shared with him some of the basics of doing Bible studies for coaches, the subject of college coaches (compared to junior and senior high school coaches) came up. Coach Hatfield definitely had thoughts about that. "Tommy," he said, "junior and senior high school coaches look up to college coaches. That's just the way it is. But, I look up to them. They're in the real battle, dealing with parents, hormones, teaching classes, and very low pay for very long hours of work. I always, always encourage my players who are thinking about coaching someday, to consider high school coaching since they will have a longer time to have a real influence in their players' lives."

LEARNING ON THE WAY

Some things you learn on the way. As Scott said, we learned that Coaches Outreach functioned best utilizing laymen—those not in full-time ministry—to facilitate our Bible studies. I say facilitate because CO designs the lessons to be self-taught, so our Lay Leaders (LLs) simply facilitate a discussion with the coaches.

But to find the right Lay Leader, we've learned to rely heavily on the grace of God. We have an application form with questions designed to help us see the heart of the man who would lead the study.

Although not necessary, many of our LLs have been in sports and already have a high respect for coaches. As flexible as we are regarding their experience in sports, we do have some strong boundaries. For example, we do not allow fathers to be Lay Leaders at the school where their child is involved in sports.

It's pretty obvious why, since favoritism could come into play.

In a similar way, since we are a non-denominational, para-church ministry, we do not allow ministers to be Lay Leaders. However, doctrinally, we would likely line up with any conservative, Bible-believing, evangelical denomination.

Across the years, great friendships have developed between Lay Leaders and coaches. Coaches discover a trusted local friendship outside of coaching, which is valuable and really somewhat rare for them.

Through God's grace, we have many hundreds of men across the country serving as Lay Leaders. There's no way to find that many great Christian men who love their coaches, and are equipped to lead the studies, without God's complete blessing.

But we've learned to be careful and cautious along the way. Early on, there was an incident that taught us a lesson…

A father, who was also a Lay Leader, confronted a coach for not playing his son more. We didn't realize this father had a son on the team. This can happen, but it can be harmful to a ministry like ours.

So, I knew this incident had to be settled—right away. I called the father and told him we couldn't have a Lay Leader angry at a coach. And I told him that we would have to find another person to serve as Lay Leader.

He became angry, but I had to stick to my decision. I called the head coach he confronted and asked for a meeting. The first thing I said, not finding another way to say it, was that I fired the Lay Leader. The coach smiled, but I didn't. I was upset, so

I tried to cool off and apologize to the coach. The coach was very gracious. I asked him to trust us to find another Lay Leader. He gave me the OK. And, I can report that we've had a study at that same school for 16 years now. God tests us sometimes, and like the slippery places on the old football fields, we might lose our footing here and there, but eventually we learn the lesson and move on.

WHY DON'T WE HAVE NOTES?

If Bible studies are the heart of Coaches Outreach, the CO "Playbook" serves as the heart of the Bible studies. We knew we wanted each coach to have a study guide, rather than just listening to what the leader had to say. We printed up handouts for each coach, but at this point, all groups studied different Bible books and topics, which, looking back, wasn't the best idea.

Around 2003, I worked with a seminary student, Cory Kuhn, to find the best way to equip coaches to grow in God's Word. This led to the first Bible study guide, with Scripture and questions, but without the answers or study notes. That was about to change.

A new group started up with some coaches in Grapevine, outside Dallas. We met in an Edwin Watts golf store. Coaches would get there a little early to have some putting contests before the study began.

As they entered, I handed out their notes, while I used the

Leader's notes—the notes with the answers. I'd be ready for the kind of probing questions for which coaches are famous. But I wasn't ready for the question one coach asked me.

Coach Kevin Atkinson looked at my notes, then glanced at his notes. Once he realized what I had in my hand—the answers—he hit me with this: "Hey, Tommy, why can't we have your notes, so we can have the right answers?"

BUILDING THE PLAYBOOK

Everyone chuckled at Kevin's question, but that question was a Godsend, and kicked us in the direction of the Playbook we use today (see an example on the previous page). These printed, spiral-bound booklets are so practical and beneficial for everyone.

Since groups meet weekly, each week's study is divided into four days, centered on a passage of Scripture. As I'm writing, our current study is *Call Out! A Study of Selected Psalms*. Each two-page day covers a portion of that week's study, Psalm 1, for example. As the Psalm is read, there are corresponding questions related to the passage. It's a simple process, to read the Scripture and answer the questions, but it kicks off the study at the surface and then goes progressively deeper.

The three categories of questions cover:

Observation (What does the passage say?)

Interpretation (What does the passage mean?)

Application (How does it apply to my life?)

My Dallas Seminary professor, Dr. Howard Hendricks, trained us to ask these questions of every passage in the Bible. So, by applying these questions to each daily passage, our studies don't just teach coaches about a particular passage—they show how to study any passage in the entire Bible.

After the questions, we provide the study notes for the passage, so everyone can have the perfect or near-perfect answer. Just what Coach Atkinson was looking for.

And, as I said, I've always told the coaches I visited, if they faithfully did the work in each Playbook, in just a few years, they'd have way more Bible knowledge than anyone else in their church! Because, it's true...coaches love competition.

Across the years since 2000, the new Playbooks have become better and better. Not just the content, but the look of the book improved, with sharp, attractive covers to pull in the coach. Our current writer, Mark Chalemin, does a great job of offering in-depth Bible study, presented in a way that new believers or seasoned saints will find insightful and inspiring.

Coaches Outreach releases two Playbooks every year—each one at the start of the new semester. The Playbooks focus on either a book of the Bible or a very significant portion of a book.

From the very beginning and to this very day, our ministry goal has always been to introduce coaches to the entire Bible. That means we study both the Old Testament as well as the New Testament. We also study all the different kinds of Bible books—stories (Genesis), letters (Ephesians, Galatians), poetry (Psalms), and prophecy (Revelation). In our study notes, we provide in-depth background, combined with life-level application suited for longtime or relatively new believers, young people to older people, and especially busy coaches.

And, despite their extremely long hours and high stress levels, many high school coaches don't make a lot of money. Some may shy away from the $10 we charge for the books, so we give them to any coach in the study. Thanks to the faithful commitment and generosity of our donors, we can provide these materials absolutely free of charge to the many thousands of coaches we serve.

NOT FOR COACHES ONLY

The Playbook drives every Coaches Outreach Bible study. But the coaches who participate function as the ministers within the group setting. By that I mean, for the most part, each person in attendance reads something from the playbook and/or offers their thoughts in response. There's no pressure, some guys talk a lot, some guys do more listening. It's real fellowship, the kind you find in the body of Christ.

Each week, coaches rub shoulders with other coaches who share the same enthusiasm, challenges, defeats, and victories. They gain a valuable, unique circle of friends, studying, learning, laughing, and praying together.

And by the way, our studies are not "for coaches only." After all, isn't a dad, or a granddad, a husband or a wife, or anyone who follows Christ and is involved with other people, basically a coach? I've heard it many times: "you're always coaching someone." So, even though the study carries a practical application to coaches in particular, the counsel and challenge in the Word of God applies to anyone and everyone.

So let me invite you to sample what CO can add to your everyday life. Scan the QR code and explore Coaches Outreach. Look over a sample Playbook you can view and download on any computer or mobile device. And check out www.coachesoutreach.org to see everything the ministry has to offer you. I believe you'll be glad you did.

213

ASK TOMMY NELSON

Any history of Coaches Outreach would be incomplete without asking my friend, Tommy Nelson, Pastor of Denton Bible Church, to jump into the game, for what radio personality Paul Harvey used to call "the rest of the story." Here's Pastor Tommy, reliving his memories of Coaches Outreach. Get ready. He loves to tell it like it is!

THE BEGINNING OF A MINISTRY
From Tommy Nelson

I knew about Maxwell as an athlete since he was famous. When I was at Dallas Seminary, I had a class in Church History. Tommy got up to hand out some papers, and I turned to the person next to me and said, "That guy's an athlete." Another time, I saw him reach for something, and I noticed a great big Super Bowl ring. I said, "That guy's a real athlete." Later on, he brought his beautiful wife, Janice, to class. I looked at her and I looked at Maxwell and I said, "That guy's a great athlete."

Sometime after that, I saw him walking across campus, called him over, and introduced myself. We started talking. Tommy shared an idea he had. I heard it and I knew he had something. "That'll work," I told him, "because it's simple. It's coaches—exclusively coaches—but without the coaching tension. And it's somebody from the outside, a teacher, with a curriculum." I advised him to start and watch how it turned out.

I knew it would work because Coaches Outreach was like a very simple Model T Ford. There wasn't anything complex about it. It was simple: leader and curriculum. And coaches. And it had Tommy Maxwell's credibility. Everybody knew the name "Tommy Maxwell." If he said it, they'd listen.

When Tommy told me he wanted to recruit Lay Leaders, I immediately thought of Scott Henderson. Scott was so personable. He was born for small group ministry. For this kind of ministry, you don't want a lecturer; you want someone who can just talk and get guys to open up. He was a natural at that. And so, Scott became the first—and the model—Lay Leader.

Sometime later, Tommy asked me to be on his board and I said yes. I wanted to see that ministry succeed. Because, really, the coach is the modern priest. If I wasn't a minister, I'd want to be a coach. But I was one of the early speakers for Coaches Outreach, because I knew I could speak to coaches. From my football days, like Maxwell, I know what a coach is, how they think, and I know they can have struggling marriages. I wanted to help.

As I look at the success of Coaches Outreach, I think it's due in part to having the right people in the right positions. Starting with Tommy himself. Really, this is one of the reasons the ministry has exploded across the country: they respected Tommy Maxwell's gift, which, let's face it, was not exactly in the realm of administration. He did what he does best. He's a people-guy. He leads with encouragement. Just like a coach, he wants to help people be more than they think they can be. He worked hard at raising up Bible studies and let other guys turn

215

the cranks. Tommy was the force behind it. He met with coaches and potential leaders and made sure he had great people surrounding him. Then watched as God grew the ministry. That's how it should be.

IMPACTING COACHES AND COMMUNITIES

Tommy Nelson is what I (Maxwell) call a "coaching pastor." Coaches work to make athletes better. Pastor Tommy won't let you get by just floating along (like that blimp); he's going to push you to give 100% to the Lord. He would get behind our pro-active mission statement:

Coaches Outreach exists to impact communities through Christ-like leadership of coaches transformed by biblical truth.

Coaches Outreach has continued to impact coaches and communities. It continues to expand, through Field Reps, Lay Leaders, and by word of mouth. By one coach talking to another coach. Or maybe, by you reading this little book.

In fact, if you're a coach in a CO Bible study, why not reach out to a fellow coach and bring them with you as a guest? Or, if you're looking for a Bible study like ours, or you might be interested in leading one as a Lay Leader, log on to www.coachesoutreach.org and let them get in touch with you.

AT MAXWELL'S HOUSE

It's Tuesday morning, 8:30 a.m., 2022. I've been retired from Coaches Outreach since 2016, but my mission and ministry hasn't changed.

In an hour, CO Bible study guys from all walks of life will step through my door, Playbooks in hand, and gather around the kitchen island to get donuts and a cup of coffee.

They'll sit around our dining table and we'll chitchat for a while, then get down to business. I'll look over at Brad Mills' Playbook and see, yep, he's got his answers and his thoughts written down, ready to go. It's a great group of guys. Brad's a retired manager from the Houston Astros. A couple of former Minnesota Vikings linemen are there (you'll know 'em when you see 'em), several retired business leaders, a pastor, two construction men, my next-door neighbor, and others.

I'm at the head of the table, and I have my Playbook highlighted with important points I want to elaborate on. Ron or Don usually opens us in prayer, and we'll dig into Day 1.

Though I'm retired, I keep leading this group, and I don't plan to stop. I love it. It's grown through the years, and just a few weeks ago, Brad Mills started a new CO Bible study with coaches in a nearby town. But he still comes to our group. Once you start into one of our studies, you get hooked. And often, hooked for life.

INTO THE FUTURE

I still do interviews about Coaches Outreach. I'll get a call, or somebody will set a time and we'll sit down and talk about it. I was at an Oakland Raiders reunion a few weeks ago and did an interview about Coaches Outreach for a podcast. I guess I haven't really left, have I?

It's fun. I get to tell my favorite stories, especially the Super Bowl V story, and field all kinds of questions. Here are two of the questions I was asked recently, and how I answered those questions. Sometimes it's a pretty big question, like, "Tommy, what's your vision for the future of Coaches Outreach?"

My answer?

It's simple. I'd love to see a coaches Bible study in every high school in America. You know, several colleges are hosting our studies now, and I'd love to see Bible studies in colleges all across the country.

The same with marriage retreats. I think of how many marriages and careers have been transformed through these retreats. I want that transformation for every coach and spouse out there. Coaches win whenever they emphasize the basics of the game on the field. You've got to block and you've got to tackle. But you need to have a great marriage, too.

Coaches Outreach stresses the basics off the field. You've got to get into the Word of God, and you've got to make sure your marriage is strong. You've got to do everything it takes to get it there. It's basic—it's urgent.

Honestly, these are the best Bible studies I've ever seen.

I've been through seminary, I've heard a lot of great speakers, and I've seen a lot of great material. But the CO studies are among the best in the country. Coaches will learn from it. They'll become better coaches from it because it's practical. The study and the interaction will inspire coaches, who will inspire others. When you take a good look at God and his plan for you, as laid out in Scripture, it gets exciting, and it takes coaching to a whole new level. Coaches Outreach will keep on going forward—impacting multiplied thousands of lives.

"How does it feel to look back at what God's done in these recent years?"

When I look back and see how this ministry has grown, it's clear that a sovereign God is in control, reproducing this ministry over and over. This past semester, we printed 7,000 Playbooks and still ran short. We have about 800 Lay Leaders, and some lead more than one group. So, that's about 6,500 coaches who participated in the study across 20-plus states.

Now the ministry has begun to expand to other countries. And two wonderful ladies on CO's staff, Ann Ryan and Tanya Baugus, started a whole new ministry just for coaches' wives called The Reach. We're discovering that young athletes want their own CO Bible studies. So, with 20 minutes of homework, four days a week, coaches can pass on the truths they've been learning to the next generation. These things are happening because God is great. Because God is faithful.

GOD'S HAND HATH PROVIDED

When I think about God's faithfulness, one thing always comes to mind. Back at Dallas Seminary, in the chapel services, we always, always opened up with a hymn. And more than any other, as I remember it, we sang "Great is Thy Faithfulness." When I think about Coaches Outreach—past, present, and future—I think it's all about God's faithfulness. God's grace, power, and especially his faithfulness, his great faithfulness.

Great is Thy faithfulness
Great is Thy faithfulness
Morning by morning new mercies I see.
All I have needed, Thy hand hath provided.
Great is Thy faithfulness, Lord unto me.

CHAPTER 16
DEPENDING
ON THE LORD

COACH SMITH

Let's start with a story.

Back at the beginning of the ministry, I spoke to a class at a Dallas inner-city school. That led to meeting the principal, who looked like he could have been a lineman himself. He saw my Super Bowl ring and that, as usual, opened the door to bring up Bible studies for coaches. I asked the principal if I could talk to a coach. "Try going to the gym," he answered. "I believe Coach Smith (head coach—fake name) is down there. He needs what you've got."

Inside the gym, kids were playing basketball. Coach Smith was sitting by himself in the stands. I worked my way up to where he was and sat down, close to him. He never looked at me. I waited and waited.

The rebel inside me said, *I'm not leaving this bench until we talk!* But again, it was the ring to the rescue. I scratched my nose, hoping my ring would catch the light. Finally, he asked, "What do you want?"

I answered, "I'd like to talk to you about a ministry to coaches. I'm Tommy Maxwell."

I reached forward, ring on finger, in plain view, and shook his hand. He noticed. He had to ask the question. "What's that ring?"

I slipped it off my finger and handed it to him. He took it carefully and looked at every side of it. I sat there wondering what he would say. Wasn't what I expected.

He replied slowly, "Do you know what this ring is?"

I told him, jokingly, I thought it was a Super Bowl ring. He looked back at the ring, then at me, and with a coach's passion said, "This is the granddaddy of all rings. Yes, sir, this is the granddaddy of all rings!" Before I could go on, he asked, "Can you give a little talk to the kids and the coaches?"

I always had a little talk ready to go, so with kids and coaches on the bleachers, I talked about teamwork and told a funny Super Bowl story. Then it was just me and Coach Smith.

"Well, what did you want?" he asked.

I described CO to him, and the coach's Bible studies. I could tell that this tough old coach had never heard of a coaches Bible study. I sensed the principal was right. He needed it.

I asked if he thought some of his coaches might be interested. Coach Smith thought it over and said, "I may have some coaches who don't smoke or drink that might come to your Bible study."

For some reason, I took that as a real challenge and grabbed

222

this coach's arm pretty good. "Coach, I want smokers and drinkers at the Bible study."

I'll never forget his response. He looked at my hand on his arm, then back at me and said, "Well, maybe I'll come!"

ACTIVE DEPENDENCE

We all know the term "dependence." And we know people who depend on things like alcohol and smoking or worse things to keep them going. They're often driven by substances on a daily basis.

If we flip that idea around, we could say that Christians are called to depend on God for the daily needs of life. I take that one step further, having an "active" dependence on God, with the same kind of drive and continual craving the psalmist described in Psalm 42:1, "As a deer pants for flowing streams, so pants my soul for you, O God."

Some would say, "Hey, we have a free will, we're not robots, programmed to constantly think about God." No, we're not. And that's probably not humanly possible anyway. But instead of being passive, or every-now-and-then, we should be active in our dependence on God. Here's my definition:

ACTIVE DEPENDENCE—An energetic, purposeful, trusting pursuit, relying on and being controlled by the perfect help of a sovereign God.

Depending on a "near-perfect" preparation in practice will result in a solid performance at game time. I remember, playing with the Colts, Coach Don Shula would demand near-perfect perfection. We started counting how many times Coach Shula would have the offense run a play. I remember it being over nine times for one play! Active dependence requires practice; it's not usually something you get on the first try. It's something that develops over time.

Active dependence moves us away from self-centeredness and toward a total reliance on the Holy Spirit, summed up in Galatians 2:20b, "It is no longer I who live, but Christ who lives in me."

The Holy Spirit within us directs us to look at Jesus as our model. We should not be content to keep doing "little" sinful things, explained by a kind of "Hey, I'm not perfect" attitude. The Holy Spirit urges believers to depend more and more on Scripture, revealing God's truth to help us overcome our self-centered, feelings-driven weaknesses. And having embarked on this life of active dependence, we find our lives filled more and more with joy, discipline, purpose, and an eternal perspective.

Let's look at three ways to apply active dependence, a three-point message I guess, which is what you might expect from a football player-turned-pastor-turned-coaches Bible study leader.

1. Active pursuit of God's will through heartfelt prayer and Bible study.
"Your word is a lamp to my feet and a light to my path" (Psalm 119:105).

PRAYER

There are times when you pray, and other times when you really pray! I recited the Lord's Prayer every night as a kid. But not long after retiring from Coaches Outreach, I had five different surgeries, all in a row, and found myself flat on my back. Not underneath a mountain of football players, but under much more serious conditions. I battled pain, weakness, and depression.

For a while, the only way I could look was up. I prayed a lot. Why does it take major situations to make us actively seek God? To force us to depend on him? Because our nature is to be independent.

Sometime later, following surgery, Janice fell into a serious condition due to an allergic reaction to medications. She was completely out of it. I'd never felt so scared in all my life.

I lay in bed, wide awake, praying, sick with fear. Finally, God literally put me to sleep. My daughter called the next morning to tell me Janice was OK. That experience amped up my active dependence and made me understand the power of passionate prayer.

BIBLE STUDY

When I've been at my lowest point, I've always reached for my Bible. And I try to keep it nearby, usually right there on the table in the kitchen. I depend on that book! It's been a lifesaver.

I told you the Psalms comforted me in the past. Well, really, they helped me to survive!

As I write this book, the Coaches Outreach Bible study I lead, at this same table, is focusing on the Psalms. I mentioned that Playbook, entitled *Call Out! A Study of Selected Psalms.* You might want to check out this terrific study. If you're in a tough season, it will definitely help you to survive, even to thrive.

At one point in the study, we centered on Psalm 23:5, "You prepare a table before me in the presence of my enemies; you anoint my head with oil; my cup overflows." David views himself as God's honored guest—with David's enemies present as captive onlookers. The Good Shepherd protects and cares for his sheep, at all times, in every situation.

If your cup is empty my friend, God's Word—and actively depending on God's Word—will fill your cup until it overflows!

2. Active Dependence on the Holy Spirit, moving from self-centered to God-centered.

"I have been crucified with Christ. It is no longer I who live, but Christ who lives in me. And the life I now live in the flesh I live by faith in the Son of God, who loved me and gave himself for me" (Galatians 2:20).

DEPENDENCE ON THE HOLY SPIRIT

Moving from self-centeredness to God-centeredness. Hmmm. I'm not sure that happens without some kind of test or trial to bring it about as the Holy Spirit works within us. Interesting that verse begins with being "crucified with Christ." That brought Paul to a place where he could honestly say, "It is no longer I who live, but Christ who lives in me." That's active dependence in action! And we, like the apostle Paul, will think of others, not just ourselves.

I've had a long history of being humbled. I needed it! Humbled in Greek and Hebrew class. Using up all the extra money football brought me. Low on money and looking for work. Pastoring and then not pastoring. And the uphill climb of long-term recovery from so many surgeries. But those challenges forced me from prideful independence to active dependence. The gradual shift from self-centered toward God-centered may be a lifelong journey. But think of the reward. Becoming more and more like Jesus!

3. Active cultivation of great love and constant trust in our awesome God.

"Trust in the Lord with all your heart, and do not lean on your own understanding. In all your ways acknowledge him, and he will make straight your paths" (Proverbs 3:5,6).

GREAT LOVE

Let's review God's plan. Not your plan, not my plan. Go back to the first commandment. "You shall love the Lord your God with all your heart and with all your soul and with all your might" (Deuteronomy 6:5). Active dependence means actively loving and worshipping God. Not just in church, or at a Bible study, but cultivating a devotion to him that keeps our hearts tuned to God throughout the day.

Reminds me of Psalm 91:1, "He who dwells in the shelter of the Most High will abide in the shadow of the Almighty." Even the youngest, little-kid football player knows to keep his eye on the ball. That's it, in a nutshell. Keep your eyes on the Lord, our invisible yet sovereign Lord, not on the pressing circumstances or the pileup of linemen on your back!

CONSTANT TRUST

I'm very thankful that God put me with the Baltimore Colts. They were a close team with an impressive heritage. The Colts had that great Bible study every Friday night with Captain Bill Lewis. I'm thankful for my coaches, Treadway, Sturdivant, Shula, Boyd, Stallings, Madden, Bum Phillips, and others. And the great QBs like Johnny Unitas, Earl Morrall, and Ines Perez.

I could say I'm not thankful for the times my life took a downward spiral. From losing jobs to losing money to losing my health. But really, how can we not be thankful? Paul, who had plenty of reasons to be ungrateful—even bitter—wrote, in 1 Thessalonians 5:16-18, "Rejoice always, pray without ceasing, give thanks in all circumstances; for this is the will of God in Christ Jesus for you." This is actively wanting God's way, not ours.

Practice makes perfect, as they say, and I invite you to practice active dependence in your daily walk with Christ. It applies to pro football players, former pro football players, truck-loaders, insurance salespeople, pastors, etc. You get the point!

"In closing," as preachers like to say, here are some scriptures for meditation, helping to keep us actively depending on God.

ACTIVE DEPENDENCE IN GOD'S WORD

"I am the vine; you are the branches. Whoever abides in me and I in him, he it is that bears much fruit, for apart from me you can do nothing." (John 15:5)

God is the source of all good things. Operating in our own strength is a waste of time. Actively depend on Him. It's the only way to grow and mature with his blessing.

"He will not let your foot be moved; He who keeps you will not slumber." (Psalm 121:3)

Coach Bobby Boyd warned me about muddy slick spots on football fields, which I experienced firsthand. God's book, the Bible, guides us around the slippery places in life, and leads us to victory.

"Delight yourself in the Lord, and he will give you the desires of your heart." (Psalm 37:4)

I desire a Lexus SUV, but that's not a real desire of my heart. When I encourage someone, pray with a friend, or lead a neighbor to Christ, those are really the fulfilling of our hearts' desires, as we delight ourselves in the Lord.

"I will instruct you and teach you in the way you should go; I will counsel you with my eye upon you." (Psalm 32:8)

There were many times when my plans got way ahead of themselves (NSF) because I moved without godly counsel. Active dependence means seeking God's will and ways, surrounded by the Body of Christ.

More scriptures for consideration and meditation:

"For I know the plans I have for you, declares the Lord, plans for welfare and not for evil, to give you a future and a hope." (Jeremiah 29:11)

"Commit your work to the Lord, and your plans will be established." (Proverbs 16:3)

"Your word is a lamp to my feet and a light to my path." (Psalm 119:105)

"What is impossible with man is possible with God." (Luke 18:27)

"The greatest of you shall be your servant. Whoever exalts himself shall be humbled, and whoever humbles himself shall be exalted."
(Matthew 23:11-12)

"Iron sharpens iron, so one man sharpens another." (Proverbs 27:17)

"Let the wise hear and increase in learning, and the one who understands obtain guidance…" (Proverbs 1:5)

"What you have learned and received and heard and seen in me—practice these things, and the God of peace will be with you." (Philippians 4:9)

"He who finds a wife finds a good thing and obtains favor from the Lord." (Proverbs 18:22)

"However, let each one of you love his wife as himself, and let the wife see that she respects her husband." (Ephesians 5:33)

"An excellent wife is the crown of her husband, but she who shames him is like rottenness in his bones." (Proverbs 12:4)

"An excellent wife who can find? She is far more precious than jewels." (Proverbs 31:10)

CHAPTER 17

FROM TOMMY
TO COACHES

HEY COACH, COULD I HAVE A MINUTE?

The only coaching I've done is helping some golfing partners with their swing and showing grandkids how to throw and catch a football.

But I came to understand what real coaching is with the help of some of the great coaches in Austin, Texas. As we gathered for one of the first coaches Bible studies, I sat there, just listening to their "out of study" and "in study" conversations. My respect for the profession of coaching didn't just increase; it took off!

And it's continuing to soar, as I hear how much coaches are enjoying our Bible studies around the country and have been impacted in practical and powerful ways.

From the beginning, I counted on advice from key coaches to help me reach out to other coaches. These key coaches know who they are. Their friendship and encouragement kept me going. Then, in a Grapevine, Texas study around 1995, coaches told me I needed to start Bible studies for other coaches. And I took their advice.

Those Austin coaches were gifted in challenging others to believe. I heard this a lot: "You can be better than you think." I like that statement. It challenges people personally and anyone they lock in on. The above coaches locked in on me! I believe coaches are drawn to those who have potential to be better and do more.

Real coaches lay in bed at night and think about players and how to motivate them. Again, it's a very unique profession that draws committed men and women. Men and women who sign up for long hours, low pay (middle school and high school), hormones, interruptions, distractions, and angry parents who are always questioning why their kid is not playing more. The win/loss record and expectation of a championship every year doesn't help the nerves either.

Successful people who stay committed and give their all, 100%, don't tend to complain as much. They understand that giving that 100%, and even aiming for improvement, are goals just as important as winning.

They know that in sports, it takes physical giftedness and drive to succeed. That kind of drive to improve and sacrifice for their teammates will make anyone successful in the long run. Physical talent or high IQ is not necessary. There are not many jobs or activities that can prepare a young person for "life." Any sport or sports team can—with a great Christian coach.

So, naturally, the people who challenged me to start Coaches Outreach were coaches.

Whatever good I have accomplished has happened because coaches sacrificed to spend time with me and encourage me to be better. And, because they really cared, and were gifted, those coaches changed my life and many other lives with their insights and challenges.

THANK YOU, COACH

So, let me thank you in particular, coach. Whatever your level of involvement, I know you work hard, get tired, and still have to push beyond it to get the job done. Let me encourage you. Even if you don't see it, you are making a difference. That difference may show up right away in some players, or not show up until they're grown and gone, raising their own families, or coaching their own team.

I see you as the "salt of the earth and the light of the world" (Matthew 5:13-14). Especially with younger players, whose lives are still being shaped. You're planting seeds, changing lives, and helping struggling kids find the success, confidence, and fulfillment they were meant to discover. I pray that the Holy Spirit will enable you to "let your light shine before others, so that they may see your good works and give glory to your Father who is in heaven" (Matthew 5:16).

LET COACHES OUTREACH ENCOURAGE YOU

And to continue that encouragement, if you haven't already done so, please take the time to find out more about Coaches Outreach. Check out coachesoutreach.org. It is a solid Christian organization run by sharp and committed Christians who truly feel called to strengthen coaches.

Coaches Outreach exists to bless and strengthen coaches, transforming their lives, spouses, families, and their work through the transforming ministry of biblical truth. That happens through Bible studies that help coaches bring discipline, truth, and grace beyond the game. The Bible study Playbooks are written for coaches and are free to coaches participating in a Coaches Outreach Bible Study at their school, and free to coaches' spouses who request them. As I said, you can use the included QR code to get your own sample Playbook. Or if you'd like to start a CO Bible study at your school, there's info on the website to help connect you to a person to get you started.

The ministry of The Reach connects coaches' wives while filtering everyday life through the Word of God. And marriage retreats recharge marriages to return to the coaching pressures restored and refueled. In addition, we have retired coaches (representatives) in different areas who visit coaches and help them start Bible studies.

I hope you're part of Coaches Outreach or will be soon. Our Bible studies will help you see a big God as never before. Your confidence and commitment to excellent coaching will grow. And helping young people live with an eternal purpose—will be your purpose.

Coach, you have a high calling. Your ability to influence is critical in our day. You will always be known as a winning coach if you always put others first, always persevere, always give 100%, and always love your athletes. All by God's grace.

LET ME PRAY FOR YOU

Our Heavenly Father, I want to thank you for every coach we have in America and across the world. Please awaken coaches to your sovereign power in their lives. Help these called men and women to live their lives close to you and your thoughts. Help them to love their athletes as you love them. Give them great wisdom and insight for their teams as a whole, and the individual athletes that are part of their lives. Strengthen coaches through their prayers and their passion for your Word, to battle Satan in his desire to discourage your coaches and manipulate their athletes. We are trusting in you to move in the hearts of these men and women you have chosen to change their corner of the world, one athlete at a time. Amen.

Button your chinstraps!
Tommy Maxwell

CHAPTER 18

COACHES Q & A

COACH TO COACH

Coaches Outreach asks coaches from a variety of backgrounds to talk about the ups, the downs, and the challenges of coaching following God's playbook, the Bible. Enjoy these stories, and be encouraged, coach!

RON CALLAHAN
36 years coaching high school and college football

What does it mean to be a Christian coach?

To be Christ-like in all situations, a man of integrity, a man who can listen and admit you're wrong to the kids. You may not agree with school board, superintendents, parents—but always let Christ be seen. Remember it's not about wins or losses; it's about the life-journeys of these kids. Kids call me, 20 years later, because they want to keep in touch. These are the trophies.

How can a coach be an influencer for Christ?

Be an example for them to see and follow. Kids will follow that example. If you don't cuss, or yell at officials, your kids will follow that example. That's the main goal.

What are some of the ways to encourage coaches?

Listen to them. Give them a vision for what they can do. Offer to help. Commit to being 100% honest with each other. Be available to talk after a tough game.

What would you say to a coach who's ready to quit?

First thing you need to do is pray. I've said things like, "Everybody comes to this point. Maybe Christ is leading in a new direction. God has you here for a reason. Hang in there."

Was there a life-changing moment in your coaching career?

I first became a head coach at a small school. In our district, teams were ranked at their place in the state, and we were #134! Our kids were small, but they worked their tails off. In the second district game, playing on their field, we lost. The school board wanted me fired, but we still had several district games ahead. Well, we beat the #14 team, then faced the #1 team, and I thought, If we lose, I'll be packing my boxes. We won, 22–0! The superintendent congratulated me, said the board would give me one more year—then I needed to move on. We went on to win several games, actually, amazing victories. One game,

240

in front of 9,000 people, we played against a team that won State. Anyway, here's the moral of the story: keep praying, and keep your boxes packed!

How has Coaches Outreach made a difference?

When my wife and I went to our first marriage retreat, we learned what it meant to walk the Christian walk. As a coach, you walk through things you don't want to walk through, but it's amazing how you can meet the challenges—because Jesus takes them on. Through CO I learned to be a husband and a father first, then a coach.

TIM KILGORE
Head Track, Assistant Football, Mabank High School
35 years as high school coach

What does it mean to be a Christian coach?

The student sees my daily walk, and hopefully observes a faith-based, joy-filled life. I mean hearing Scripture sprinkled into my language, getting a pat on the back, giving me some sweat (chest to chest), all of this making Christian-deposits into their lives. And when you do have to make a correction, you have enough deposits to make the withdrawal. It means not having a "bankrupt relationship" with the players.

Without upfront preaching, how can you influence a player/student for Christ?

Eye contact and body language, so the kids will know you care. Pray: "Lord help me love the kids today, even the kids I don't love." It's about unconditional love, being friends with the best ones and the worst ones; it has to be all of them. Coach 'em all.

What is the state of coaching today?

Today is different. The expectations of players are different. And it's different than when I played in the 70s and 80s. Coaches still want to win, but social media has affected things. Kids and parents are promoting themselves more than anything. There's a great storm of selfishness today, and the parents are pushing it as well as the kids. Other problem: a coach's hands are often tied on discipline. Even low-key discipline. A consequence needs to have a bite to be successful. It's a challenge to be a coach today.

What do coaches need to be encouraged?

Coaches need to be constantly reminded that the scoreboard does not define them. God loves them. Really, they're coaching for an audience of One. Wives are yelling the coach's names. Ignore the fan base. This is for an eternal impact. Kids come back to me and say, "The way you walked reminds me of how I want to coach." Coaches need this wind in their sails.

How did you hear about CO?

I was coaching in Brady, Texas. Bobby Price, a pastor there, was a music leader for CO. For a wedding gift, he gave us tickets to a Coaches Outreach marriage retreat. We've gone ever since. And once we met Tommy, we were hooked. Love the in-depth teaching and fellowship of the marriage seminar. If you haven't checked it out, do it now.

How does CO help your wife?

CO recognizes two major things. One: Wives see that their husband is actually in a ministry. They want to be part of that ministry. Not a team mom, but involved. Two: They talk to other wives. Sharing the demands on the marriage, the younger wives hear advice from the older wives, sharing stories and encouragement, how to not just get through it, but contribute and be blessed. Encouraged and motivated, wives respect and support the husband. And husbands are reminded to love their wives. Get things in order: she comes first, then the career.

What is the hardest thing about coaching?

Coaching your own kids. Most difficult, but also the most fun. My son was a quarterback. He called me coach, not Daddy. During Covid, in a quiet stadium in Mansfield, I watched my son and my wife get picked on, just because he was the coach's kid. Your kids will go through some adversity. Just have to let it happen. Can't say "Quit picking on my kid." Just have to swallow the unfairness of things. And keep moving forward.

RUDY POWE
Defensive Coordinator, MacArthur High School
Coaching 28 years

What does it mean to be a Christian coach?

I have been humbled by coaching. I think I have the game—and life—all figured out, but it leaves me broken each year. Yet my brokenness is redeemed as I endure the highs and the lows with the players, through each year, game, practice, and class period. You can't take players to a place you have never been.

My faith has refined me over the years, to be the example, an imperfect man held up by a loving Savior. I'm just here to aid others in their race as I fight through my race. God breathe life into me each day as I try to breathe life into my players and students.

How can a coach be an influencer for Christ?

As a coach you're a model on the biggest stage. Eyes are on you nonstop. The kids see you as you handle the highs and lows. In the high, we give thanks; in the low, we give thanks.

What are some ways to encourage coaches?

Words of affirmation. A coach goes through so many life highs and lows during a day. When we receive a kind word, we hold on to it like a gold medal.

Coaches are true hoarders. We keep tokens of affirmations from our wives, players, and faculty. We hold on to the good in all people's actions.

What's the hardest thing about coaching?

Living your life in a fish tank or a glass house. Kids see everything you do. Your wife sees everything you do. They know who you are inside and out.

What would you say to a coach who's ready to quit?

Read your Bible; there are plenty of good people who wanted to quit. Finish the race that was set before you.

Was there a life-changing moment in your coaching career?

As I become an older coach and meet players I have coached, they repeat the things they remember about me. In my early years, I gave kids some bad nicknames, and I'm not proud of myself for that. I changed my ways immediately.

How did you hear about CO?

I was blessed in my sixth year of coaching to be on the staff of David Beaty at North Dallas High School. He was a first-time head football coach, and he was determined to have a CO Bible study with his coaching staff.

How does CO help your wife?

At the CO marriage retreat, she has an opportunity to meet "our people," people that run the same race as we do. The coaching roller coaster is not for the faint of heart. It takes a toll on your relationship. It's nice to reconnect with her and connect with people fighting the same battle. It encourages us to persevere and keep focus.

How can older coaches mentor younger coaches?

Get them into a Bible study. Get them to a CO marriage retreat. Pray for them as they are not ready for the journey that has begun.

STU JOHNSON
Defensive Coordinator, Lewisville High School
Coaching 18 years

What does it mean to be a Christian coach?

First, have your priorities in order: faith, family, then football. Surround yourself with other Christian coaches who will help hold you accountable, especially with the competitive nature of athletics. A Christian coach is one who allows the Holy Spirit to be present not only in words, but also in actions. For many athletes, their coaches may be the only positive Christian influence they have in their lives, so we need to strive to grow our relationship with Christ constantly and model that in the way we coach. Be vulnerable and show humility when we make mistakes, letting our athletes know that we are human and not perfect and capable of sin. However, through Christ we are redeemed.

How can a coach be an influencer for Christ?

Humility. When I was younger, I felt that I wasn't good enough to be a Christian—I thought I needed to be perfect. We show our athletes we are not perfect—and they don't have to be either. We all put our faith and trust in the Lord. Look for opportunities to speak about Christ. I ask if I can pray for them. After praying with them several times, they usually begin to ask about Jesus. These are the moments to be bold and speak the Truth. Let them know your beliefs. Use words and actions to show how much you love and care for them. This builds trust, and models the Christian life, especially when so many outside influences work to drive them away from Christ.

What are some of the ways to encourage coaches?

We encourage coaches the same way we encourage athletes, with humility, selflessness, service, and love. The way we handle ourselves daily as Christians impacts everyone around us. We have to speak boldly about our faith with other coaches. It can be difficult, it's a must.

What's the hardest thing about coaching?

For me, it's the time away from my family—especially during your sports season. That's why it's so important to have a wife that understands the impact you have on the young men and women you coach. At times it seems you're around them even more than your own family. That's why I often bring my family to the school. I want the players to see my Christian faith in action and observe the positive interaction—and love—between me, my wife, and my son.

What would you say to a coach who's ready to quit?

I start with asking questions about their purpose. I try to find out if they're coaching as a job, likely as a non-Christian—or as a Christian, wanting to impact young people's lives. If a coach wants out, I want to know why they want out. From the job point of view, it's understandable. They want more time with family, need more money, get tired of the pressure, etc. From the Christian point of view, when they see it as a ministry, I encourage them to stick with it, because even with the demands and difficulties, they're making an eternal difference.

Was there a life-changing moment in your coaching career?

First, being baptized at 25 years old, during my first year coaching at Mesquite. I had a bunch of the players from the same church that showed up for the service, cheering as I came out of the water. I knew my life had been changed and that my influence as a Christian coach could have far-reaching impact.

Second, last year, we had a large number of football players get baptized. It started with one of our leaders making that decision, which was the result of our staff being the positive

Christian influences he needed. This led to many more players making the decision to accept Jesus as their Lord and Savior.

How did you hear about CO?

Two of my college coaches brought me down to Texas and we were coaching together at Mesquite. They invited me to the CO Bible study, but I was reluctant, since I hadn't made a personal decision to accept Jesus. However, they were persistent, and I joined, and later made my decision to follow the Lord. I began helping them with FCA and eventually took over as the FCA huddle coach. Since then, I have been a part of every CO study and have served as an FCA huddle coach every year.

How does CO help your wife?

She knows how important CO is to me and she sees the impact it has, not only on my coaching, but in being the Christian man I strive to be daily.

How can older coaches mentor younger coaches?

Build a relationship with younger coaches. They usually take on a lot of extra duties; stepping in to help can really encourage them. Invite them to CO if they aren't already attending. CO is one of the most important things I do every week. If something comes up and I have to skip the study group, my whole week feels like it's missing something. If the younger coaches see our selflessness and humility, while knowing we are active members of CO, it will encourage them to join as well, and that is the greatest thing you can do as a mentor.

THERESA URBANOVSKY
Judson High School Softball Coach
29 years coaching college, high school, and middle
school

What does it mean to be a Christian coach?

The word "coach" is a description of who you are. Adding the adjective "Christian" gives a person an accountability to be like Jesus. Every action you do reflects who you are and registers with the impressionable minds of each student and/or athlete you encounter. Everything you do should be Christ-like. Your actions speak louder than words. A Christian coach values all people and strives to help each one be the best version of themselves. A Christian coach is who you are all the time.

How can a coach be an influencer for Christ?

As a coach, every day is an opportunity to display Christ in my life. My coaching staff and athletes need to see how I handle the situations I encounter. I need to be true to my values and consistent in my leadership.

What are some of the ways to encourage coaches?

Coaches often try to please everyone. But, instead of that, they need to learn to be the best version of themselves daily. Love is a key to growing as a coach. Once you allow yourself to love each one of your students, peers, and coaches, you begin to feel empathy. I empathize all the time with my athletes, so they know I am feeling the same emotions they feel. I identify with them. I call these moments "HOG" (Hand of God) moments. I have learned to cherish HOG moments, and I try not to be so caught up in distractions that the HOG moments get overlooked.

What is the hardest thing about coaching?

When your character or intentions are attacked. As coaches, we invest everything we have, we do our best, and prepare for each opportunity. When someone doubts the purity of our intentions—it hurts. When my athletes do not reach their full potential, I feel responsible. I feel I have failed them, and my influence has had no effect. But these things are all part of a coach's journey, an athlete's journey, and our life's journey in Christ.

What would you say to a coach who is ready to quit?

I would ask them why they want to quit. Then, I would dig deeper to help them understand the root of their feelings. I would ask if they have totally disconnected, to make sure they are settled with the decision to leave the profession. Sometimes, a person must walk away to appreciate their experience, or confirm it was the right decision to step away. I would just be there for a coach in this dilemma.

Was there a life-changing moment in your coaching career?

I've had several life-changing moments, but one directly hits home. In my 29 years of coaching, I've only overslept once or twice. But on the first day of our CO Bible study (17 years ago), I overslept 15 minutes. Growing up in Catholic school, I had no idea what a Bible study was like. I didn't understand the value of it. But there I was, the new person, arriving late, and I would have to face a group of male coaches whom I greatly admired: Coach Jim Rackley, Coach Melvin Boelter, Coach Rick Rhoades, and our leader, Dr. Dearl Dotson. It was a spiritual struggle. I could skip embarrassing myself and just show up the next week—or walk in late. I chose to step into the room, not knowing how the coaches would react. Each one of them welcomed me with open arms, not asking any questions. Because it was a brand-new experience, I'm sure that, if these men would have treated me differently, I would not have returned. And if that had happened, I doubt I would ever have grown spiritually. These coaches held my hand through my new Christian walk, each one making me feel like I belonged. Our CO group has weathered many storms, and we have been there for each other through our life events. This is my accountability group, companions with me through my spiritual journey. I have grown exponentially from the personal experience of my CO Bible study.

How did you hear about CO?

I heard about the CO Bible study from Coach Rhoades

who had attended the marriage retreat. He brought the information back to Judson High School and started the Bible study with our wonderful leader, Dr. Dotson.

How can older coaches mentor younger coaches?

The seasoned coaches should invite the younger coaches to opportunities like the Coaches Outreach Bible study. In that unique setting, veteran coaches share a wealth of experience, and younger coaches share in a unique fellowship outside of the game. When you separate from the game, and build trust through intimate relationships, you start to see how you can help each other personally and spiritually.

As the head coach of two of my former players who now assist me, I work hard to allow them to have a voice, and know their value. I learn from them, just as much as they learn from me. It's a special relationship. Our motto is LOVE WINS. When you genuinely love something, you will passionately give back. I want our coaches to genuinely love what they do and give back to every life they touch.

TOMMY COX
High School Coach & Athletic Director, Retired
Coaching 30 years, Austin, TX

What does it mean to be a Christian coach?

You don't coach a sport; you coach a kid. You can take a

Christian coach who only knows football and put him in a sport he's never coached, let's say, lacrosse, and he'll be successful because he's not coaching sports; he's coaching kids. And from a spiritual perspective, it's a ministry. God has placed you there to lead kids to Christ. And in this environment today, you lead them to Christ 99.9% by how you treat them and how they see Christ in you. You don't get a lot of opportunities to witness to kids today.

How can a coach be an influencer for Christ?

I've heard of a Christian teacher who took time, after school, to walk by every desk and pray for the kids who sat in those desks. So, one day I left my office and went to the locker room and sat on the bench and prayed for certain kids who were going through difficult times. Another coach talks openly about his Christian faith, challenging kids to hold him account-able to keep his faith up front. Football is competitive, so that's a tough approach to take; it has to be Christ living through us.

What are some of the ways to encourage coaches?

Coaches can get caught up in the wins and losses, but it's really about the long-term effect you can have on a player. A parent once asked, "Hey Coach, what kind of year are we going to have this year?"

The coach answered, "I won't know until about twenty years from now. When I see how these young men turn out, and if they turn out good, I'll know I made a difference, and I'll know we had a good year."

I've got a few kids that call me on Father's Day. That's in-credible. I just listened to a song called "Coach" by Kenny Chesney. He played high school football in Tennessee. The line that gets me is, "We'll never forget you, Coach." One of the kids I coached sent it to me by text, and said, "I just wanted to send this to my favorite coach."

What's the hardest thing about coaching?

You get all kinds of kids that come into your life, into the locker room, onto the field. A Christian coach doesn't just side up with the talented, obedient, easy-going kids. Or the kids that are headed for great careers in sports. You get all kinds, and you give them all your best. You've gotta love them all. Even the unlovable, the wayward child, or the Prodigal Son (Luke 15:11-32). You're gonna be successful with some and not as success-ful with others. Because none of us are perfect, by a long stretch. So, if anything good happens, with me, and coaching, it was God directing it.

What would you say to a coach who's ready to quit coaching?

I try to "blow the whistle" and get the coach to stop before making any rash decisions. It's easy to want to jump ship when the pressure is on, or the losses are piling up, or any number of things are going wrong—all at once. I encourage that coach not to make this decision based on emotions. I try to remind the coach to pray about it. Pray and keep praying. And to make sure he (or she) has buy-in from their spouse. Scripture instructs us to seek wise counsel from trusted believers, like family, coaches, educators, and pastors. Seek the Lord, listen, and wait before you jump.

How did you hear about CO?

Tommy Maxwell led the first coach's Bible study for about four years. I was in that group, and when I was coaching at Bowie, Tommy came to my office. He wanted to share his vision for CO. He later put together our first summer conference at T Bar M. Tommy was concerned about filling all the spots, so our coaching staff at Bowie helped with that, and I think we had eight couples attend. A great beginning!

How does CO help your wife?

Brenda loved the conferences. The worship and fellowship was great, and our presenters were excellent. They focused on how to love your spouse, sharing biblical principles (and applications) for a successful marriage within the coaching environment. She also noticed that studying God's word on a regular schedule with my peers made me a better husband and father to my sons.

How can older coaches mentor younger coaches?

For active, mature coaches I would say live out your faith. Let them see you loving kids. Sponsor a Bible study for kids and/or coaches. Ask God to make you available to these younger coaches. When they see what you are doing, they'll ask you how you got there.

BRAD MILLS
MLB Manager, Retired
Coaching 32 years

What does it mean to be a Christian coach?

Christian coaches, hopefully, realize that they have fallen short (sinned), and so has each person on their team. In knowing this basic truth, the coach can care for each player as an individual, on level ground, rather than just a person the coach "uses" to get things done, or to perform, or to rack up points.

When this takes place, hopefully a relationship can form that helps everybody pull in the same direction. Does this happen 100% of the time? HA! Our pride gets in the way and, even though we start out in the right direction, we often lose focus and start spiraling out of control.

Wish I could say I did it right in every circumstance, but the truth is, for most of my coaching career, my focus was on the wrong thing! I hope that, in 40 years of baseball, playing and coaching, I've learned to care for each individual, seeing them as Christ, through grace, sees us.

How can a coach be an influencer for Christ?

By everything the coach does: behavior, speech, actions, etc. Is it possible to be this way in every situation? Probably not, but it's impossible unless we are filled with the Holy Spirit.

257

Even then, it's challenging, and can be extremely difficult. Some have had that kind of success. John Wooden and Tom Landry are a couple that come to mind. Success as an influencer for Christ comes through prayer, study, and ongoing fellowship with Christian coaches.

When I was coaching, I made it a point to talk to each team member at every practice. If I forgot, or missed somebody, they wondered if I was upset about something! That was a small thing to do, but sometimes small things can make a big difference.

What are some of the ways to encourage coaches?

Telling and showing coaches that they are cared about. Spending as much time with them as possible, showing you're interested in them and not just trying to get things from them.

What's the hardest thing about coaching?

The first thing that comes to mind is having the right kind of discernment—about everything—on a daily basis. When you're wrong, admit it, and have humility. And when things aren't going well, take responsibility. These things make you a leader, the kind your players will want to follow.

What would you say to a coach who's ready to quit coaching?

The first thing I would ask would be, "What were your expectations going in?" Coaching is tough. Being intentional with everything you do is hard and exhausting—but extremely important. I'm sure more questions would come up as the conversation continued, hopefully providing some clarity as the coach makes his decision.

Was there a life-changing moment in your coaching career?

When I came to the realization that everybody—the players, coaches, front office, owners, even the crowd—all want and need the same thing. Each person needs confirmation that they matter, that they're important. Sometimes that confirmation can come in the simplest ways, such as a hello, a smile, or just not brushing them off. Sometimes it comes in sharing some coaching advice, praying together, and sometimes just a look or a wave from a distance. However it's given, it's so important—for all of us—to know we matter. To know we're needed.

How did you hear about CO?

I was just asked to come to a Bible study and wanted to be supportive of men seeking the Lord. Now I try not to miss it. And I'm starting up a new CO Bible study in another town.

How can older coaches mentor younger coaches?

By just being their friend and supporter, setting up a relationship that's not affected by losses or wins. By being a good listener, and only giving advice if asked. That shows you care about them and aren't coming across like a know-it-all. Mentoring means loving someone for who they are, not for who you want them to be. It's like unconditional love, and it can open the door to sharing your faith with them.

EPILOGUE

GOING FROM
DOWN TO UP

THAT KID AT THE CONFERENCE

Walking with the Lord can bring great moments. High
points, when you realize he really is close! And the other kind
of moments. Low points.

At this time, I was at a low point in my life—maybe the
lowest.

I told you about my season as a pastor, and how I had received some, shall we say, "exit papers." In the middle of that
"time out," friends in Denton invited us to come visit them.
We knew they attended Denton Bible Church.

I knew the pastor there, Tommy Nelson, and we were anxious to take a getaway. After the service, a young man (Keith
Chancey, on staff at DBC as youth minister) came up and introduced himself. I didn't recognize him at first.

He said he was that teenage kid who was always by my side
at a conference where I oversaw about 10 young guys. We

261

would compete against other teams in different sports. Then I remembered him, but I didn't know the whole story.

Keith said he had a note I'd sent him after the conference. I remembered writing and sending that note, but I didn't know much it meant to him.

Not only did he keep it—he framed it. And kept it right there on his desk.

You can read that same story, but from his perspective, as he tells it, below.

But, that day at Denton Bible, hearing him talk about the framed note on his desk—that really touched me. It's hard to explain how I felt. I can still feel that moment 30 years later. In a split second, I went from "down" to "up."

Traveling to Denton, visiting the church, and meeting Keith Chancey, now a youth minister, really flipped things over. A low point became a high point.

I thought, in good times, in bad times, we are still close to God. More importantly I guess, God is always close to us. And always in charge.

As my friend Scott would say, "There are no coincidences. God is in control."

And I add, "And we know that for those who love God all things work together for good, for those who are called according to his purpose" (Romans 8:28).

A LETTER BACK TO TOMMY

From Keith Chancey

To the man who helped change my life: Tommy Maxwell. What an incredible story! Here was a kid out of Dallas who came to an FCA conference in Estes Park, Colorado—where Tommy Maxwell had just had surgery on his leg. A kid who was seeking something...desperately needing the Lord but not knowing that's what I needed. Angry at life and angry at God because my dad had abandoned my family, I was looking for anything that would give me comfort.

At the conference, Tommy said to me, "Chancey, why are you so mad? Tell me the object of your anger." So, I began to tell him about my dad who had abandoned my family and gambled away every penny my family owned.

I told Tommy how alone I was, and how I blamed God for that. Tommy said, "God didn't do that. Man did that." He explained salvation to me, how God had a plan for my life, and how man is the sinner and God is the Redeemer.

From that day forward, I was never the same. I always look back and say that's the moment in my life when God used a man to help me understand the truth of God.

The joy of that is, when I got back in 1975, Tommy sent me a letter explaining how I needed to live my life now. From that day, I have had that letter framed on my desk or mounted on my wall. It's gone with me to every place that I've moved, every office that I've had. I want to be able to look at it and think, *that's the moment God changed my life*. He used a man—

Tommy Maxwell—who came into my life.

And I'll never forget how Tommy said to me, the day he led me to Christ, "Chancey, I want you to go play football and I want you to go rewrite the record books."

Well, you know what? When I got home from that conference, I had a letter from Ouachita Baptist University. I opened it and I called the coach and said, "Coach, I'm gonna to come to your school and I'm gonna rewrite your record books."

The rest is history because the record books that God used me to rewrite turned out to lead several of my teammates to Christ. Rewriting the record books, Tommy helped me to understand, wasn't necessarily playing sports but making an impact for Jesus Christ.

Tommy Maxwell, it was a pleasure for me to write this note for you because you were influential in helping me understand how to live life and live it to the fullest. May God be with you. Thank you.

COACHES
OUTREACH

Coaches Outreach exists to impact communities through
Christ-like leadership of coaches transformed by biblical truth.

coachesoutreach.org